THÉOPHILE-ALEXANDRE STEINLEN

Front Cover:
Young Woman of the Street, ca. 1895, oil on canvas (cat. 227).

Back Cover:
Cafe Scene, ca. 1920, watercolor (cat. 119, volume 3).

Frontispiece:
Figure 1. *Self-Portrait,* illustration for *Le chat noir,* 6 April 1895, photorelief.

THÉOPHILE-ALEXANDRE

Steinlen

PHILLIP DENNIS CATE
and
SUSAN GILL

Gibbs M. Smith Inc.
Salt Lake City

This is a Peregrine Smith Book.
Published by Gibbs M. Smith Inc., P.O. Box 667, Layton, UT 84041.

Book design by Adrian Wilson.

Library of Congress Cataloging in Publication Data
    Cate, Phillip Dennis. Steinlen.
    Catalog of a retrospective exhibition.
    Includes bibliographical references and index.
    1. Steinlen, Theophile Alexandre, 1859-1923—Exhibitions.
    2. Social problems in art—Exhibitions.
I. Steinlen, Theophile Alexandre, 1859-1923.   II. Title.
N6853.S8A4   1982   760'.092'4   82-5816
ISBN 0-87905-129-9   AACR2

Plate 1. Cafe Scene, ca. 1920, watercolor (cat. 119, volume 3).

Cat Reclining on a Rectangular Stand, ca. 1904, bronze (cat. 237).

To Norma Bartman and Margot Flatau

Cat, no date, color stencil (cat. 173).

Contents

Figure 2. *Drunkards,* cover illustration for *Le mirliton,* November 1888, stencil colored photorelief (cat. 124).

HERSCHEL B. CHIPP

Introduction

Since 1977 numerous exhibitions and catalogues in western and eastern Europe have dealt with the art of Théophile Alexandre Steinlen, a name only superficially known in the United States. A Montmartre avant-garde artist along with Henri de Toulouse-Lautrec, Pierre Bonnard, and Edouard Vuillard, it was he whom the public knew best, his work that drew the most critical recognition, and his influence that suggested new directions to such American artists as John Penfield, John Sloan, and Edward Hopper and to such Europeans as Pablo Picasso, Käthe Kollwitz, and Georges Braque.

The 1980 tidal wave of interest in turn-of-the-century posters which sent the auction and gallery prices sky-high, and dropped them just as dramatically in 1981, had the positive effect of establishing Steinlen as a major poster artist of *la belle époque.* Color postcards reproducing his posters became popular and Dover published his cats and his 1890s illustrations from *Gil Blas illustré.*

This exhibition and publication hope to reveal to the American public the richness and variety, not only of Steinlen's art, but his many roles in the social and artistic environment of *fin-de-siécle* Paris as postermaker, printmaker, painter, sculptor, and illustrator of journals and books. They also hope to provide a comprehensive and balanced view of his double-sided art: its social-political content and highly personal and even humorous imagery.

Between the mid-1880s and the turn of the century, the masters of modern art forged the forms and techniques that would shape all the arts of the twentieth century. Simultaneously, Art Nouveau, following the liberating trends in social and political thought, provided for a brief period a brilliant alternative to the conventions of mainstream art. Old prejudices against the graphic arts toppled. Popular illustrations and prints became technically challenging and legitimate areas of the fine arts. Original drawings could be cheaply reproduced on a printed page and even augmented with color (fig. 2).

In 1881, France passed a law granting freedom of the press, and an explosion of little magazines of humor, comment, and social criticism resulted. Posters could appear in public places as long as they were clearly distinguishable from official notices and were confined to designated locations. Daring and provocative ideas circulated freely, and for the first time since the art of Daumier and Courbet, the faces and doings of Paris's common people were featured, usually anecdotally but sometimes heroically.

Figure 3. *In the Vincennes Woods,* cover illustration for *Le mirliton,* April 1892, stencil colored photorelief (cat. 125).

Paris was an explosion of fireworks, an energetic and energizing center for the arts. Théophile Steinlen, trained and apprenticed as a fabric designer in Switzerland, could have become a central figure in the Parisian fashion industry when he arrived in Paris in 1881 at the age of twenty-two. But the colorful spectacle of the common people on the boulevards and side streets at the foot of Montmartre proved to be too appealing. Quickly drawn into the circle of artists, poets, and musicians at Rodolphe Salis's new cabaret in Montmartre, the Chat Noir ("Black Cat"), he became a close friend and collaborator with the star of the show, poet and singer Aristide Bruant. Steinlen first illustrated Bruant's rowdy songs when published as sheet music. Bruant later established a little magazine named after his own cabaret, Le Mirliton ("The Toy Flute"), for which Steinlen also did illustrations (fig. 3).

Steinlen's drawing style for his street people focused on characteristic gestures and faces without the specificity of portraits, and he often isolated a central mass of figures against the whiteness of the paper. Only occasionally did he devote much attention to the setting.

By the decade of the 1890s, Steinlen began to move beyond his romantic, even idealized figures of promenaders on the boulevards, lovers in the park, and housewives at the markets. The prolonged depression and political unrest turned Steinlen to illustrate strikers and demonstrators on the march and rioters for Paris's radical journals.

Most of the artists of Steinlen's generation, particularly the Neo-Impressionists, struggled with the opposed demands of aesthetic qualities and a clear social message in their political art. Much of the period's work on social themes has been dismissed as effective "propaganda," but not quite "art." Steinlen, however, had the gift of extracting social meaning from a specific human situation; thus, the viewer is struck first by a convincing drama, which is strengthened by the quality of the drawing, and is then led to consider larger ideological conclusions. Thus, apparently without theorizing on the problem, Steinlen continued Daumier's tradition: a vigorous drawing style expressing his deep sympathy for human situations which in turn capture broader social meanings. It was perhaps this characteristic of Steinlen's art that influenced other artists rather than his specific style or choice of subjects. The young Picasso was profoundly influenced by Steinlen and would later make his own artistic contribution to social themes.

Because of the appeal of his art and because of its wide distribution in popular journals, Steinlen became the best-known illustrator of the 1890s throughout Europe and America. Largely through his drawings in Le chat noir and Le mirliton magazines, the cabarets for which they were named became known as the center of the vivacious, sophisticated, and critical life of Montmartre. He made close to seven hundred drawings for two weeklies, Gil Blas illustré and, later, L'assiette au beurre, which established him as a leading social critic and humorist. Georges Braque, questioned in 1954 about his artistic education, replied simply, "I did it all alone with Gil Blas." Electrified by Steinlen's and Toulouse-Lautrec's illustrations at about twelve years of age, he spent his evenings copying them.

The foreign artists who looked most eagerly to Paris for guidance were the Cataláns of Barcelona, the cultural capital of Spain and the Paris of the peninsula. The literary and artistic movement called "Modernismo" was Montmartre transplanted and translated. Its leader, Santiago Rusiñol, as an art student, had haunted the Chat Noir cabaret where he had admired and been influenced by Steinlen, Toulouse-Lautrec, and Jean-Louis Forain. Another Spanish art student and "Modernismo" leading light was Ramon Casas, whose portrait subjects included Eric Satie, then the pianist at the Chat Noir, in a vigorous style like Steinlen's. Both Rusiñol and Casas spent a few months each year doing familiar scenes already depicted by the Montmartre artists (fig. 5). Back in Barcelona these paintings were avidly studied. Miguel Utrillo came as a correspondent for La Vanguardia and,

Figure 4. Cover for *Dans la rue,* 1895, color lithograph (cat. 37).

entranced by the shadow theater of Henri Rivière at the Chat Noir, produced similar shows at Barcelona's version of the cabaret, Els Quatre Gats ("The Four Cats"), in 1897. After Rusiñol and Casas established themselves in an apartment in the Moulin de la Galette and divided their time between Paris and Barcelona, other Spanish artists followed. Joaquin Sunyer, still in his teens, read his poems at the Chat Noir while he lived literally in the streets of Montmartre. Isidro Nonell and Ricardo Opisso arrived during the years of political turmoil and focused on victims of the depression and unemployment. Although the Spaniards' work was more melancholy and lacked the verve of the Frenchmen's, Nonell's drawings were published in *Le rire* and *Frou-frou* and his paintings were widely shown.

In Barcelona Els Quatre Gats was the gathering place of the leading artists and poets. Their own magazine, *Els Quatre Gats,* later succeeded by *Pel y Ploma,* gave them a forum to celebrate Catalán culture. Their ideas and work inflamed a younger generation, whose ages averaged about twenty years. All of them, including Picasso and Carlos Casagemas, eagerly planned their own pilgrimages to Paris. The Paris periodicals were always on the tables, filled with the drawings of Steinlen, Toulouse-Lautrec, and Forain.

Picasso's first drawings and paintings of Paris show that he saw the city through those French illustrated periodicals. When Käthe Kollwitz came to Paris, she wanted first to see Rodin and then to visit Steinlen. Her lithographs for *The Weavers,* 1896, show a shared concern with Steinlen on social issues and also a similar graphic style. Susan Gill's essay on Steinlen's social and political subjects document Steinlen's impact on Spanish and American artists who either expressed admiration for his social thought or were stylistically influenced.

Steinlen continues to be a refreshing well for artists. He seems to have resolved the technical and moral dilemmas that make some artists choose form and others content, fueling the never-ending debate between art and propaganda. In Steinlen's balance of these two conflicting demands may lie his greatest significance.

Figure 5. *The Bread Carrier,* 1892, oil on canvas (cat. 222).

Plate 2. *Rodolphe Salis at the Chat Noir Cabaret,* ca. 1884, watercolor (cat. 217).

PHILLIP DENNIS CATE

I

Steinlen and His Art: A Chronological Survey

Jadis Watteau rassemblait dans l'ombre fine et dorée d'un parc des compagnies qui, sous les frissons du satin, parlaient d'amour. Aujourd'hui les arbres des parcs sont coupes et ce qui s'offre à l'artiste ému, subtil, impatient d'exprimer la vie et le rêve de son époque, c'est la rue, la rue populeuse. Une sensibilité subtile, vive, attentive, une infaillible mémoire de l'oeil, des moyens rapides d'expression destinaient Steinlen à devenir le dessinateur et le peintre de la vie qui passe, le maître de la rue. Le flot clair et matinal le flot sombre et nocturne des ouvriers et des ouvrières, les groupes attablés sur le trottoir, que le mastroquet appelle alors la terrasse, les rôdeurs et les rôdeuses des noirs boulevards, la rue enfin, la place publique, les lointains faubourgs aux arbres maigres, les terrains vagues, tout cela est à lui. De ces choses il sait tout. Leur vie est sa vie, leur joie est sa joie, leur tristesse sa tristesse. Il a souffert, il a ri avec ces passants. L'âme des foules irritées ou joyeuses a passé en lui. Il en a senti la simplicité terrible et la grandeur. Et c'est pourquoi l'oeuvre de Steinlen est épique.[1]

(Formerly, Watteau gathered in the refined and golden shadow of a park companions who, under the shiver of satin, spoke of love. Today the trees of the park are trimmed and what offers itself to the inspired, keen artist, impatient to express the life and the dream of his time is the street, the populated street. A subtle, live, attentive sensibility, an infallible visual memory, some rapid means of expression destined Steinlen to become the draughtsman, the painter of passing life, the master of the street. The bright morning stream and the dark nightly stream of male and female workers, the groups at outdoor cafés, the male and female vagrants of the dark boulevards, the street, at last, the public square, the remote suburbs with barren trees, vacant lots, all that is known to him. Their life is his life, their joy is his joy, their sadness his sadness. He has suffered, he has laughed with these wayfarers. The soul of the bothered or happy crowd has passed in him. There he has felt terrible simplicity and grandeur. And that is why Steinlen's art is epic.)(fig. 6)

1. Anatole France, preface to the catalogue: *Exposition d'ouvrages peints, déssinés ou gravés par Th. A. Steinlen* (Paris: Edouard Pelletan, 1901), pp. 11-12.

STEINLEN.

Dupont. sc.

Figure 6. P. Dumont, *Portrait of Steinlen,* ca. 1900, wood engraving. Courtesy Jane Voorhees Zimmerli Art Museum.

This statement, made by no less an authority than Anatole France in the preface of the catalogue for the 1903 Steinlen Exhibition in Paris, makes a grand claim. Yet it is not unjustified. Steinlen had, in twenty years, created an art that was epic not only in his range of subjects and ability to perceive the "terrible simplicity and grandeur" of the common life but epic also in its sheer public visibility over time. More than any other artist of the time, he had harmonized his art to the new rhythms of economical printing techniques with the result that it had reached thousands upon thousands of people weekly on the covers of a variety of magazines, popular sheet music, and books, as well as on the buildings of Paris.

The 1903 exhibition at 32, place Saint George revealed Steinlen literally in midcareer, halfway between his first illustration for *Le chat noir* journal in 1883 and his death in 1923. He was also at the peak of his artistic activity. The score of years before the exhibition had seen ninety percent of his lifetime's printed work: posters, illustrations, book covers, etchings, and lithographs. His reputation as an artist of the people, as a socialist, and as a realist was secure. His pictorial art paralleled and often illustrated the work of such literary and social realists of the period as Emile Zola, Jean Richepin, Guy de Maupassant, Jehan Rictus, and, by the end of the 1890s, his close friend Anatole France. All these harsh revelators sought to rip away the polite masks protecting the comfortable middle classes from the plight of the common man, the injustices of the bourgeoisie, and the even greater fundamental inequalities which western society ceaselessly engendered.

Although Steinlen's work extended beyond World War I, he was most notably an artist of the 1880s and 1890s. Like such independent young artists of the period as Jean-Louis Forain, Adolphe Willette, Caran d'Ache, Henri Ibels, and Henri de Toulouse-Lautrec, Steinlen rejected outright traditional salon painting, Impressionism, and Post-Impressionism; most often he concentrated his efforts on printmaking and illustrating for

Figure 7. Honoré Daumier, *Laundress on the Quai d'Anjou,* ca. 1861, oil on wood.
Courtesy Albright-Knox Art Gallery.

magazines and books, thus recording both witty satires of contemporary street life, the *café-concert,* and the boudoir, and also with outraged humanity, a scathing criticism of social injustice. The height of his political involvement came during the peak of the Dreyfus affair in 1897. Thus, socialist artists returned to the tradition of realist artists/journalists like Thomas Rowlandson, Gavarni, J.J. Grandville, and Honoré Daumier who translated the specifics of daily life into universal human conditions.

19

Figure 8. *Interior of a Street Car*, 1896, lithograph (cat. 39).

Steinlen's art of humor and of protest followed directly in the tradition of Daumier. Often in subject and in style the younger artist relied heavily on the paintings, drawings and prints of his predecessor (fig. 7-9).

The two artists shared a certain aptitude for the graphic arts—drawing and lithography, in particular. Both were prolific illustrators and social/political commentators. Although they both painted and sculpted with success, their drawings and prints seem primary; and in my opinion, their greatest artistic strengths most consistently lie in their graphic work. Although their lives overlapped twenty years, Steinlen never knew Daumier personally, for he did not arrive in Paris until two years after Daumier's death in 1879.

Théophile Alexandre Steinlen was born in Lausanne, Switzerland, on 10 November 1859. His father, Samuel, was an official at the local post office, while his grandfather, Théodore Christian Gottlieb Steinlen, had acquired a reputation as a landscape watercolorist in Vevey, a town just southeast of Lausanne on Lake Leman. From 1810 to 1849 his grandfather worked as a lithographer at the print shop Klausfelder, where in 1833 he produced an album of lithographs depicting the costumes and decorations associated with the festival of wine makers. Steinlen's paternal uncle Marius also worked as a painter of enamels at the studio of Charles Gleyre in Paris. The young Steinlen therefore grew up, if not in an environment of art, at least with drawing, painting, and printmaking as part of his family background.[2]

As a youth he revealed a strong predilection for drawing, a sensitivity toward nature, and a concern for animals, which, as he matured, broadened into an overall humanistic view of life. He attended, without great enthusiasm, the University of Lausanne, between 1876 and 1878. His father finally realized that his son's real interest was art and sent him to Mulhouse, a textile center in

Figure 9. *The Laundress,* 1894, oil on canvas (cat. 233).

Alsace-Lorraine, directly west of Paris, to combine his talent with a practical occupation.

There Steinlen apprenticed in the textile factory of Schoenhampt and produced original woodblock designs to be printed on fabric. It was also in Mulhouse that he met Emilie, his future wife. In 1881, the two traveled to Paris and set up their household on Montmartre where Steinlen found employment in an Alsatian fabric factory.

2. For a more complete biography of Steinlen see Maurice Pianzola, *Théophile-Alexandre Steinlen* (Lausanne: Editions Recontre, 1971).

Plate 3. *Bread Carrier,* 1895, pastel (cat. 190).

Figure 10. *The Windmills of Montmartre,* 1903, oil on canvas (cat. 230).

Paris, and especially Montmartre with its crowded mass of impoverished humanity, must have been a revelation to Steinlen. The dark side of Montmartre had been the focus of Emile Zola's sensational 1877 book *L'assommoir* ("The Trap"). Steinlen had read it and had been greatly moved by its detailed description of the pain of urban poverty and the helplessness of the two protagonists, Gervaise and Coupeau, to avert either their alcoholism or their doom. His social awakening dates from that reading. In 1900 Steinlen would create a poster to advertise the play based on Zola's book, but his art throughout much of his life was often the graphic equivalent of *L'assommoir* (plate 10).

From 1881 until his death, Montmartre was Steinlen's home as well as his subject (fig. 10). In December 1881 another Swiss expatriot, Rodolphe Salis, founded the Chat Noir cabaret at 84, rue Rochechouart in the heart of Montmartre (plate 2). The following January, he began publishing *Le chat noir,* a weekly periodical. For the next fifteen years, Salis's two black cats represented the spirit of anti-establishment intellectuals and artists. Salis was a forceful, persuasive showman who was also a bit of a poet, artist, politician, and con man. He not only served as host and master of ceremonies at the cabaret and often wrote in and illustrated his magazine, but also,

23

LE CHAT NOIR

Le Roman d'un Peintre. --- Dessin de Steinlen.

Figure 11. *The Story of a Painter,* illustration in *Le chat noir,*
6 September 1884, photorelief (cat. 122).

in 1884, ran for municipal office on the platform of separating Montmartre from Paris! Salis and his friends represented a wry new spirit characterized by a special brand of self-indulgent humor: puns, in-jokes, and the absurd. This humor was translated into the sophisticated impudence of the illustrations by Adolphe Willette, Caran d'Ache, Henri Rivière, and eventually, Steinlen himself (fig. 11). The Hydropaths, a group of poets and composers

under the leadership of Emile Goudeau, became the poets in residence at the cabaret. Goudeau organized Friday and Saturday literary *soirées* as well as Wednesday literary absinthes at which Salis introduced the performers.[3]

The magazine and the cabaret performances were fresh, witty, satirical, political, literary, and international in content. By 1885, the popularity of the Chat Noir outgrew the building and, on the evening of 10 June 1885, in a comical musical procession, Salis and his entourage moved to 12, rue Laval (today rue Victor-Massé) (fig. 12). It was there, in 1886, that the artistic director of the magazine, Henri Rivière, initiated his famous Chat Noir shadow theater performances, and it was at that location, until Salis's death in 1897, that the cabaret attracted the cream of Parisian artists, writers, and composers. Toulouse-Lautrec, in an 1886 letter to his mother, recorded:

> *Je me suis fort amusé ces jours-ci au* Chat noir. *Nous avions organisé un orchestre, et nous faisons danser le peuple. C' était fort drôle, seulement on se couchait à 5 heures du matin, ce qui fait souffrir un peu le travail dudit matin.*
>
> (I've been having a very good time lately here at the Chat Noir. We organized an orchestra and got the people dancing. It was great fun only we didn't get to bed until five in the morning which made my work suffer a little that morning.)[4]

In 1887-88 Salis published *Le chat noir guide,* which included a list of the cabaret's diverse participants. It contained such artists as Pierre Puvis de Chavannes and Edgar Degas; such diverse authors as Emile Zola, J.K. Huysmans, Edmond de Goncourt, Jules Verne, Alexandre

3. For further discussion on the Chat Noir see: Mariel Frèrebeau, "What is Montmartre? Nothing! What should it be? Everything!", *ARTnews* 76 no. 3 (March 1977): 60-62; and *Centenaire du chat noir* (Paris: Musée de Montmartre, 1981).

4. Lucien Goldschmidt and Herbert Schimmel, *Unpublished Correspondence of Henri de Toulouse-Lautrec* (New York: Phaïdon Publishers Inc., 1969), p. 101.

Figure 12. *An Evening at the Chat Noir Cabaret*, ca. 1895, photograph.

Figure 13. *Dispute de filles,* 1895, lithograph (cat. 34).

Dumas, François Coppée, and Anatole France; scientist Louis Pasteur; engineer of the Panama Canal Ferdinand de Lesseps; photographer Félix Nadar; art critic and collector Philippe Burty; and controversial journalist Henri Rochefort among others.[5]

Steinlen was first introduced to this intensely varied, richly artistic, and anarchic environment of the Chat Noir in 1883 by Adolphe Willette. There Steinlen associated with songwriters, composers, and actors like Aristide Bruant, Maurice Boukay, Paul Delmet, and Mounet Sully; with the publishers Ernest Flammarion, Paul Ollendorf, and A. Quantin; with writers like Zola, Rictus, and Richepin; and with artists like Rivière, Auriol, and Willette. These artists were to become his collaborators, lifelong friends, and/or social-political comrades. Just as important, however, was Salis's invitation to Steinlen to contribute illustrations to *Le chat noir,* and it was within those pages on 1 September 1883 that Steinlen's artistic career, however hesitantly, was launched.

In 1913, Ernest de Crauzat, writer, collector of prints, and a member of the Society for the Propagation of Art Books, prepared a *catalogue raisonné* of Steinlen's printed work, which the Society published. This major undertaking contains 745 detailed and annotated entries which document several thousand individual printed items. Although there are some omissions, it is a surprisingly accurate and essential reference of the first thirty years of the artist's career. It places in sharp contrast the lack of documentation of the last ten years of Steinlen's life. Unfortunately, Crauzat's catalogue was published in a relatively small edition of 575 and therefore is not always readily accessible.[6]

5. *Le chat noir guide* (Paris: Le chat noir, 1887-88), pp. 60-64.
6. Ernest de Crauzat, *L'oeuvre gravée et lithographiée de Steinlen,* (Paris: Société de propagation des livres d'art, 1913).

Figure 14. *The Last Ambush,* 1894, stencil colored lithograph (cat. 25).

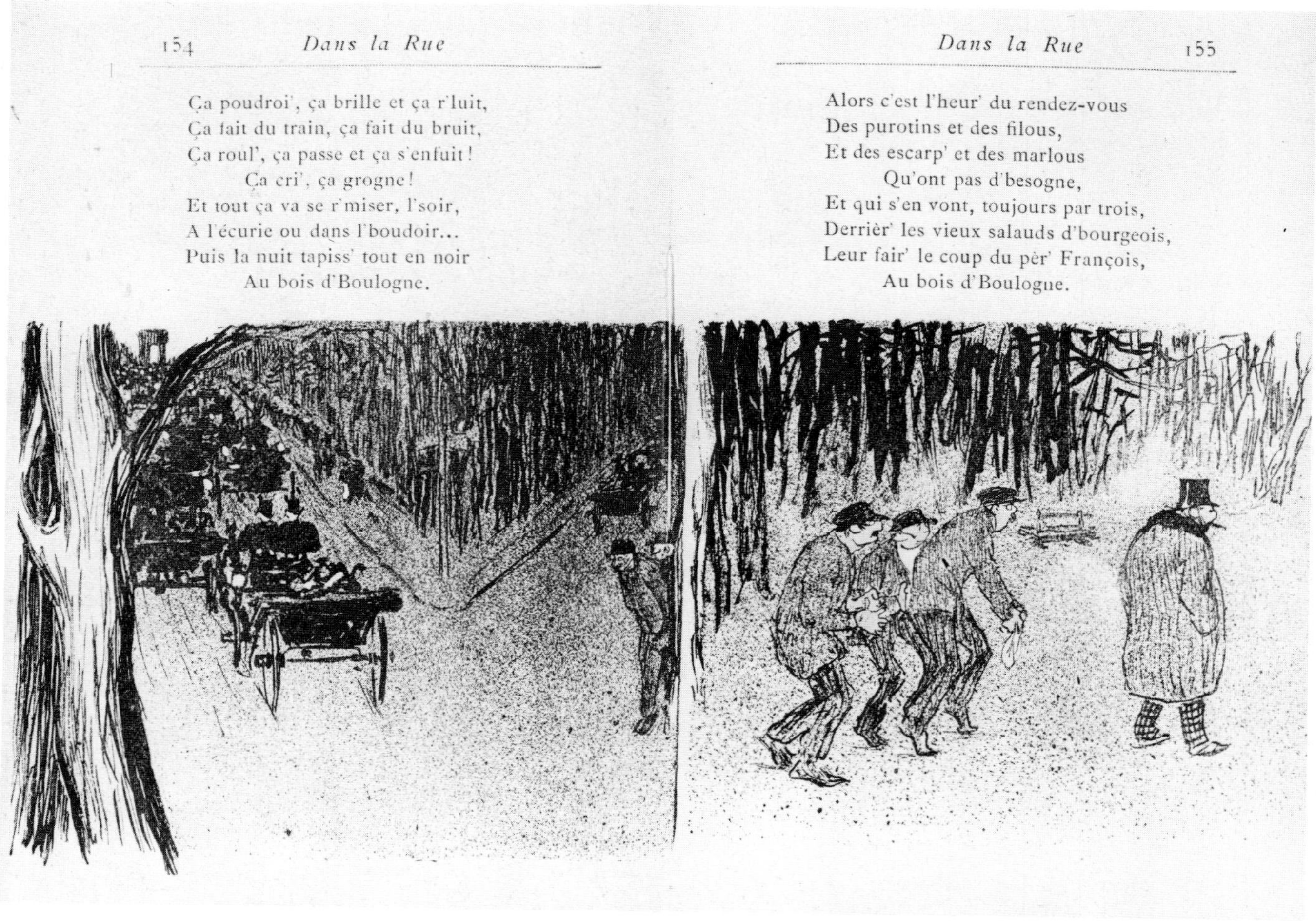

154 *Dans la Rue*

Ça poudroi', ça brille et ça r'luit,
Ça fait du train, ça fait du bruit,
Ça roul', ça passe et ça s'enfuit!
Ça cri', ça grogne!
Et tout ça va se r'miser, l'soir,
A l'écurie ou dans l'boudoir...
Puis la nuit tapiss' tout en noir
Au bois d'Boulogne.

Dans la Rue 155

Alors c'est l'heur' du rendez-vous
Des purotins et des filous,
Et des escarp' et des marlous
Qu'ont pas d'besogne,
Et qui s'en vont, toujours par trois,
Derrièr' les vieux salauds d'bourgeois,
Leur fair' le coup du pèr' François,
Au bois d'Boulogne.

Figure 15. *Au Bois de Boulogne,* illustration in *Dans la rue,* 1895, photorelief (cat. 104).

Crauzat's catalogue used the following sequence of categories:

I. Original Etchings (C.1-115)

II. Monotypes (C.116-126)

III. Original Lithographs
Lithographic Prints (C.127-296)
Lithographic Sheet Music Covers
(C.297-480)
Lithographic Posters (C.481-517)
Books Illustrated with Original
Lithographs (C.518-519)

IV. Works Illustrated with Steinlen
Designs, Usually Using
Photomechanical Reproduction
Individual Prints (C.520-523)
Sheet Music Covers (C.524-535)
Book Covers, Books, and Albums
(C.536-648)
Magazines and Reviews (C.649-704)
Prospecti of Books and Journals
(C.705-713)
Programs (C.714-720)
Exhibition Announcements (C.721-724)
Invitations and Menus (C.725-735)
Miscellaneous Illustrations (C.736-745)

Even running the eye down these categories reveals that the majority of Steinlen's work was practical: his drawings served as commercial sheet music covers, book and magazine illustrations, posters, announcements, etc. An even closer evaluation of the 170 "original lithographic prints" (C.127-296) indicates that these too, with rare exceptions, such as *Dispute de filles* ("Arguing Prostitutes") (fig. 13), were produced for a particular project—either to accompany a text like the album, *Chansons des femmes* ("Songs of Women") (fig. 16) or for future reproduction in journals, such as the thirty-two lithographs reproduced in *Le chambard socialiste* ("The Socialist Riot") (fig. 14). Even though the original lithographs for *Le chambard* were printed in a limited edition of one hundred, they were typographically reproduced in the same size and stencil-colored on the cover of this journal which boasted a circulation of 50,000.

Figure 16. *Drinking Song,* illustration for *Songs of Women,* 1897, photorelief (cat. 108).

The majority of Steinlen's art was created to be reproduced photomechanically for mass circulation. Crauzat included 519 entries under all the categories of "original" prints and only 226 entries under the categories of reproduced work, but there are actually more than 2,000 items in the second category and about 600 original, etched, monotyped, and lithographic images in the first. Of these 2,000 items, most were taken from drawings Steinlen made specifically for photomechanical reproduction in books, such as the two volumes of *Dans la rue* ("In the Street") (fig. 15) and in periodicals such as *Gil Blas illustré* (the weekly illustrated

29

Figure 17. *Bittersweet,* drawing for cover illustration for *Gil Blas illustré,* 28 February 1892, pen and crayon (cat. 180).

Two Coachmen"), which appeared in the 3 July 1886 *Le chat noir,* was again reproduced in the November 1899 issue of *Cocorico* ("Cockadoodledoo"). Illustrations for *Le mirliton* and the two volumes of *Dans la rue,* printed in large trade editions, appeared again in books about and by Aristide Bruant, the popular cabaret singer. Examples included Oscar Méténier's *Aristide Bruant,* 1892 (cat. 98), *Chansons et monologues,* 1896-97 (C.588), *La lanterne de Bruant,* 1897 (C.593), and *Les types de Bruant* ("The Characters of Bruant"), 1902 (cat. 116). In 1901, one hundred Steinlen illustrations from *Le chat noir, Le mirliton,* and *Gil Blas illustré* were brought together in the book *Dans la vie* ("In Life") (cat. 144).

Figure 18. *The Robber Robbed,* illustration for *Des chats,* 1898, photorelief (cat. 111).

supplement of *Gil Blas*)(fig. 17). In other instances, such as the publications of *Histoire du chien de Brisquet* ("The Story of Brisquet's Dog")(cat. 113), *L'affaire Crainquebille* ("The Crainquebille Affair")(cat. 114), and the journal *L'image* (cat. 239), wood engravings were made from Steinlen's drawings by craftsmen such as Ernest and Frédéric Florian.

Steinlen's designs were also reproduced over and over again in a variety of publications, giving his work widespread exposure. His humorous "stories without words" first illustrated *Le chat noir* of the 1880s, but later appeared in two albums, *Des chats* ("Some Cats"), 1898 (fig. 18) and *Contes à Sarah* ("Stories for Sarah"), 1899 (cat. 112). *Les deux cochers* ("The

Figure 19. *Exhibition of Drawings and Paintings by T.A. Steinlen,* 1894, color lithographic poster (cat. 75).

The bulk of Steinlen's printed work was very public and nonelitist, a practice which coincided with his social philosophy. As such, his work was a direct link between the general populace and the art world. While he associated with the avant-garde artists of the 1890s, he rarely exhibited with them. Unlike his colleagues at the Chat Noir, Steinlen did not participate in the major limited edition group-print publications, such as André Marty's *L'estampe originale* ("Original Prints"), 1893-94, and Ambroise Vollard's *L'album d'estampes*

originales de la Galerie Vollard, 1897. Approximately one hundred contemporary artists were represented in these albums.

Why was Steinlen omitted? It was certainly not because he was unknown. A large one-man exhibition of his work was hung in 1894 at the Galerie Bodinière (fig. 19). He had established himself as a poster artist and a printmaker, and, in fact, his work was published and distributed by Edouard Kleinmann, an important dealer for the young avant-garde, who also promoted the prints and posters of Toulouse-Lautrec, Henri Ibels, Willette, Jules Chéret, Forain, Rivière, and others. Did the editors find his political views repugnant? Unlikely. Featured artists like Maximilian Luce and Henri Ibels had similar views. Luce had, in fact, spent time in prison in 1894, at the peak of anarchist terrorism. Was his work too plebeian? Also unlikely. The designs of Chéret and Forain, both included, were also widely published. Did Steinlen exempt himself from these "arty" efforts for philosophical reasons? No more plausible. One of his lithographs was included in Löys Delteil's short-lived, rather conservative, 1896 publication, *L'estampe moderne*. Another appeared in the album of the same year, *Étude des femmes*, which also included work by Toulouse-Lautrec,

Georges de Feure, and Félix Vallotton.[7] Steinlen also had a collotype or photolithographic reproduction from his drawing, *Bal de barrière* ("Dance on the Outskirts of Town"), included in the June 1898 issue of a third successful, limited-edition publication, also called *L'estampe moderne* (fig. 20). This last album published four prints monthly for two years in editions of 150, interspersing photoreproductions of drawings by some artists among actual lithographs by other artists; however, each work was

7. *Etudes de femmes* consisted of twelve prints in four installments by Hermann-Paul, Toulouse-Lautrec, Willette, J.E. Blanche, Paul Helleu, Maurice Moreau-Nelaton, Eugène Carrière, Puvis de Chavannes, Valloton, Chéret, Georges de Feure, and Steinlen. It was published by Le livre vert: L'estampe originale and printed by Lemercier in 1896.

Figure 20. *Dance on the Outskirts of Town*, 1898, colored collotype (cat. 90).

Figure 21. *Those in Luck's Way,* proof for cover illustration in *Le mirliton,* 2 February 1894, stencil
colored photorelief (cat. 128).

Figure 22. *Belleville/Menilmontant,* illustration for *Dans la rue,*
1888, photorelief (cat. 93a).

designated "original." Perhaps it was precisely this merging of mass-produced art and limited edition prints which appealed to Steinlen. Certainly it was the pattern he had followed in creating a limited-edition lithograph, which was usually mass-produced photomechanically to illustrate such periodicals as *Le chambard* and *Le mirliton* or such trade edition books as *Chansons des femmes* and *Chansons de Montmartre.* In addition, proofs of these photorelief reproductions of the lithographs were printed on special paper to be sold to collectors (fig. 21). Such versatility gave Steinlen access not only to the small collector but also to his mass audience.

Only a few of his publications were aimed specifically at the limited edition market, all of them after 1900 when his reputation was well established. Anatole France's *L'affaire Crainquebille,* 1901, illustrated with sixty-three engravings from drawings by Steinlen, was printed in an edition of 400 on special paper (cat. 114). Guy de Maupassant's *Le vagabond,* illustrated with fifty-one lithographs, was printed in 1902 in an edition of 150 for the Society of Friends of Books (C.518). Richepin's *La chanson des gueux* ("Song of Tramps") and *Dernières chansons de mon premier livre* ("Last Songs of My First Book") were published in 1910 in editions of 340 and 330 respectively, with illustrations produced photomechanically from Steinlen's drawings. Three examples of each of these Richepin books were printed on Whatman paper and bound with proofs of each illustration on japan and china paper plus numerous original drawings and/or watercolors (plates 1,16).

Beginning in 1904 and continuing until the end of his life, Steinlen carved approximately one hundred designs into special leather bindings of rare, proof volumes of *L'affaire Crainquebille, Le vagabond, Barabbas* by Lucien Descaves, and the *Chansons* volumes by Richepin, as well as various others' works (plate 4).[8]

8. Crauzat, "Les 'Incises' de Steinlen," *Plaisir de bibliophile* no. 1 (Feb. 1925): pp. 26-34.

Ya des fois qu'i's font du potin,
I's japp', i's piss', i's font des magnes...
Dam' les clebs i's ont pas des pagnes
Pour plumer avec leur putain.

Et comme en somme i's som pas d'bois,
I' faut qu'i's fass'nt ça dans la rue,
Sous les yeux d'la foule accourue
Et des bons sergots aux abois.

Figure 23. *The Four-Footed,* illustration for *Dans la rue,* 1895, photorelief (cat. 104).

These unique, precious volumes stood in sharp contrast to the inexpensive, easily accessible, large edition paperbacks of *Dans la Rue* on which Steinlen and Bruant collaborated beginning in 1888. Yet they revealed not a snob, but a craftsman. They were an art form in their own right. For the most part, he concentrated on the challenge of designing a book artfully yet inexpensively. The integration of his drawings with the text of Bruant's songs in the *Dans la rue* volumes was one of the high points of *fin-de-siècle* innovative book design (fig. 22,23). The two volumes of *Dans la rue* were also published in a limited edition on japan paper, often with pen and ink drawings, poems, and signatures added by

Figure 24. Title page for *Dans la rue*, 1888 (cat. 94).

Steinlen and Bruant (fig. 24). The creation of the two versions added to the evidence of Steinlen's versatility.

A brief summary of Steinlen's artistic career may begin with his most public art, his periodical illustrations, and finish with his most private, the etchings.

From 1883 to 1911, according to Crauzat, Steinlen's illustrations appeared in fifty-six magazines and special supplements. Except for *Simplicissimus* (C.673) and *Altravers Gli Albi et le Cartelle* (C.698), German and Italian publications respectively, these were all Parisian magazines. However, those he dominated and which gave him the greatest visibility were: *Le chat noir, Le mirliton, La caricature, Gil Blas illustré, Le chambard socialiste, Le rire* ("The Laugh"), *La feuille* ("The Leaf"), *Cocorico, L'assiette au beurre* ("The Butterplate"), and *Le canard sauvage* ("The Wild Duck"). *L'été* ("Summer"), Steinlen's first illustration for *Le chat noir*, appeared in September 1883. It was an uninspiring debut; nevertheless, the following February, his humorous and slightly gruesome "stories without words," dedicated to Sarah Salis, the young daughter of Rodolphe, were initiated. During the following seven years, Steinlen contributed to a total of ninety-two issues of *Le chat noir*, with his participation dwindling each year from the high point of twenty-five illustrations in 1884. This slow but steady reduction was countered by his progressively greater involvement with other journals, such as *Le mirliton, La caricature,* and *Gil Blas illustré.*

From 1883 to 1885, Bruant regularly entertained at the Chat Noir, developing an abrasive aggressive style which brought him great popularity among Left Bank sophisticates who came to the cabaret to relish Bruant's insults, gutsy recitals, and sweetly sentimental laments for pimps, prostitutes, and thieves. His songs were of street people—the very criminals, drunks, whores, and tramps who inhabited Montmartre—sung in the argot of the street. They circulated rapidly among the bistros and the unsavory parts of the city, and he soon became their *chansonnier populaire.*

Steinlen first collaborated with Bruant in the 9 August 1884 issue of *Le chat noir*; he illustrated Bruant's *La ballade du chat noir,* dedicated to Salis. When Salis moved the Chat Noir to larger quarters in June 1885, Bruant took over the old building and established his own *café-concert, Le mirliton,* where for twelve years he continued to abuse his delighted customers (fig. 25). Following Salis's example,

L'intérieur du *Mirliton* (dessin de Steinlein).

Figure 25. Interior of Le Mirliton Cabaret, illustration for *Dans la rue,* 1895, photorelief (cat. 104).

Figure 26. *Half-Beavers,* cover illustration for *L'echo de Paris,* ink and crayon (cat. 185).

Bruant began to publish his cabaret's journal, *Le mirliton,* in the fall of 1885 (cat. 124-128). For ten and a half years, it appeared irregularly, sometimes monthly, sometimes biweekly. It existed primarily to publicize Bruant's songs, although later, in 1892, it developed into an organ for all Parisian *café-concerts.* Illustrators included Henri Pille, Heidbrinck, Steinlen, and Toulouse-Lautrec. Steinlen used a pseudonym, Jean Caillou ("pebble," the French equivalent for the German *stein,* "stone"). Toulouse-Lautrec appeared as *Tréclau,* obviously the transposition of *Lautrec.* In 1894 and 1897-99, for his illustrations in the socialist *Le chambard* and *La feuille,* Steinlen used another pun upon his name: *Petit Pierre* or "little stone."

Still collaborating with Bruant on *Le mirliton,* Steinlen also began illustrating covers for *La caricature* and *L'echo de Paris* in 1890 and 1891, respectively, with a repertoire of images and themes similar to those developed in *Le mirliton* (fig. 26). It was, however, the pages of *Gil Blas illustré,* beginning in July 1891, that saw his most prolific work (cat. 129-134). He created close to 700 designs for its front and back covers in a decade. *Gil Blas* offered the opportunity of collaborating with numerous realist writers and poets, and his repertoire of themes of contemporary life expanded enormously. Steinlen's developing style and maturing themes could best be traced in the pages of *Le chat noir, Le mirliton,* and *Gil Blas.*

If it was in *Le chat noir* that Steinlen first developed a predilection for humorous satire, it was with *Le mirliton* that his humor is first combined with his compassion for the people of the street, and with *Gil Blas* that his collaboration with the realistic school of

Plate 4. Incised leather book bindings highlighted with color for Jean Richepin's 1910 edition of *The Beggars' Song* (cat. 119, 3 volumes) and of *Last Songs* (cat. 120).

Figure 27. *Two Honest Women*, drawing for cover illustration *Gil Blas illustré*, 8 May 1896, ink and crayon (cat. 194).

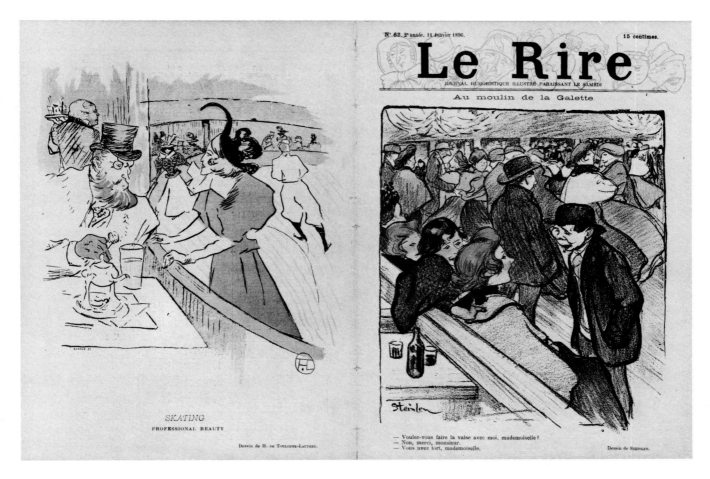

Figure 28. Back and front covers for *Le rire*, 11 January 1896, color photorelief (cat. 135).

literature was first realized (fig. 27). However, it was the covers of thirty-two issues of *Le chambard* in 1893-94 that most passionately displayed his anti-capitalist views. In *Le rire*, 1896 and 1897, humorous and satirical illustrations by Steinlen appeared along with those, among others, by Charles Léandre, Willette, Félix Vallotton and Toulouse-Lautrec (fig. 28). However, the revival of the Dreyfus affair in 1897 aligned Steinlen with the political left and he created seventeen harsh full-page satires for Zo d'Axa's *La feuille*. He did not revert after the termination of the Dreyfus affair, and, from 1901 to 1905, created

Le 18 Mars au Père Lachaise: — Qu'est-ce que c'est, m'sieu l'agent, une société d'anciens militaires?
— Non, c'est le reste des insurgés qu'on a oublié de fusiller en 1871.

Figure 29. *March 18th at Père Lachaise Cemetery,* drawing for *Le canard sauvage,* 21 March 1903, chalk and wash (cat. 198).

numerous illustrations for *L'assiette au beurre* (fig. 30) and, in 1903, *Le canard sauvage* (fig. 29) dealing with a variety of injustices and ironies. Steinlen did all the illustrations for two numbers of *L'assiette*: the 11 July 1903 special issue, *14 Juillet,* and the 14 November 1903 issue, *Les deux justices* ("The Two Justices"). This period proved to be the last of his great journalistic contributions.

Steinlen's large-edition popularly illustrated sheet music covers, books, and albums in all media—lithography, photomechanics, etc.— number close to three hundred and essentially date from 1884 to 1912. *Le portrait de Jules,* a photomechanical color illustration for *Imagerie artistique,* 1881, is a rare and unusually early work by Steinlen that Crauzat missed (cat. 145). Except for a postcard based upon the poster design of *Journée du poilu* ("The Day of the Doughboy"), Steinlen's post-1913 work appears devoid of such ephemera (cat. 157).

Figure 30. *The Issy Catastrophe,* cover for *L'assiette au beurre,* 27 June 1901, color photorelief (cat. 141).

Figure 31. Cover for *Dans la rue,* 1888, stencil colored photorelief (cat. 93).

Figure 32. *Flirt,* 1892, color lithographic sheet music cover (cat. 65).

Book covers and books saw him create approximately one hundred photomechanically printed illustrations, which range from humorous to sentimental and from satirical to social-political. His most popular works, however, were the two volumes of *Dans la rue,* Bruant's flamboyant collections of songs and monologues. Bruant published the first edition in 1888 (fig. 31). It contained thirty-one of Bruant's most popular pieces, such as *A Montrouge* ("At Montrouge")(fig. 33), *Marche des dos* ("Walk of the Rebels"), *Amoureux* ("In Love"), *Belleville-Menilmontant,* etc. These earthy verses in argot were accompanied by 113 designs by Steinlen which overlap and integrate with the text and the music or serve either as vignettes or as separate full-page illustrations.

Figure 33. *At Montrouge,* drawing for illustration for *Dans la rue,* 1888, (cat. 177).

Between 1884 and 1900, Steinlen created 184 lithographic designs for sheet music covers—during the 1880s, primarily with Bruant. These designs sometimes also appeared on the cover of *Le mirliton.* His activity in this field peaked between 1889 and 1895 when he worked not only with Bruant, but also with many other composers and poets, including Marcel Legay, Maurice Boukay, Paul Delmet, and Alphonse Daudet. He created close to 150 popular sheet music covers that were published by *La semaine artistique et musicale,* by Henri Rochefort's *L'intransigeant illustré,* and by the editors G. Ondet and A. Fouquet (fig. 32).

Plate 5. *Louise Michel on the Barricades,*
        ca. 1885, oil on canvas
        (cat. 218).

Plate 6. *The 14th of July,*
        1895, oil on canvas
        (cat. 226).

Figure 34. Cover for *Red Songs*, 1897, color lithograph (cat. 109).

Figure 35. *The Dream,* 1891, color photorelief printed poster (cat. 91).

The second volume of *Dans la rue,* published in 1895, contained thirty new songs and monologues (cat. 104). Such rabble-rousing songs as *A Mazas,* the tale of a thief in Mazas prison, and *Au Bois de Boulogne,* an analysis of the advantages and disadvantages of seeking prostitutes in the famous park on the western outskirts of Paris, received vivid treatment from Steinlen's 148 illustrations. Thousands of copies of the book were published, thus promoting to an even wider audience than that of the Mirliton cabaret and its journal the songs of Bruant and the art of Steinlen.

His lighthearted books of 1897-1900, such as *Chansons de femmes* and *Chansons de Montmartre,* illustrated with photoreductions of lithographs, and his books for children, *Des chats,* 1895, *Contes enfantins* (C.601), and *Contes à Sarah,* 1899, contrasted sharply with his socially-conscious work at the turn of the century in *Chansons rouges* ("Red Songs"), 1897 (fig. 34), *Les soliloques du pauvre* ("Soliloquies of the Poor"), 1903 (cat. 117), and *Les gueules noires* ("The Miners"), 1907 (cat. 118).

Crauzat recorded a total of thirty-seven color lithographic and one color photomechanical poster that Steinlen created for outdoor display between 1885 and 1906 (fig. 35). There was an additional untallied number produced after Crauzat's publication. Steinlen's first nine posters, printed prior to 1890, advertised in a very academic style a hotel at Trouville-sur-mer, baths in the western Pyrenees, biscuits, rat poison, cough drops, etc. The development of his own style really began in 1893 with *Mothu et Doria,* a poster advertising two cabaret performers. In the subsequent sixteen years, Steinlen's posters, advertising such diverse subjects as Yvette Guilbert (plate 21), sterilized milk (plate 20), cocoa and teas, bicycles (plate 16), novels, and health foods (cat. 88), used essentially the same visual vocabulary as Steinlen's work for magazines, books, and sheet music. In his advertisement for sterilized milk, for instance, he depicted his young daughter, Colette, surrounded by the ever-present Steinlen cats. The cat reappeared in his poster for cocoa and teas, in the Chat Noir cabaret posters, and in an advertisement for a veterinarian clinic (fig. 36). An over-size poster advertising Charles

Figure 36. *Chéron Veterinary Clinic*, 1905, color lithographic poster (cat. 87).

Figure 37. *The Tenant,* 1913, color lithographic poster (cat. 149).

Verneau's print shop was a colorful scene of a Parisian crowd. That advertising the stage version of *L'assommoir* was an interior of a typical Steinlen bistro (plate 10). The product advertised became absorbed in and sometimes secondary to Steinlen's strong style and distinctive imagery.

In 1913 with *Le locataire* ("The Tenant"), a poster advertising the publication of a tenants' federation, Steinlen's posters began promoting social causes rather than commercial products (fig. 37). His war posters showed evicted and displaced Belgians forced out of their homes by the German attack or French whose cities had been destroyed by battle (fig. 39). An untitled poster of 1922 depicted a mother and two young daughters tightly huddled together within the protecting arms of the husband/father. From the background emerged the symbol of death, a skeleton with a laurel wreath and a scythe (fig. 38). Historically, such a symbol referred to famine or plague; indeed, this work may have alluded to the famine in Eastern Europe at that time. Unlike Steinlen's optimistic and even idealistic work of the 1890s, this poster was a cynical version of the world. The war had ended but it had not brought peace and prosperity. In fact, the period between the wars was filled with depression, political upheaval, repression, and finally, the renewal of hostilities. Indeed, this 1922 work may have been Steinlen's last poster. He died the following year on 13 December.

Figure 38. Untitled color lithographic poster, 1922 (cat. 172).

Figure 39. *The Social Duty,* 1917, color lithographic poster (cat. 169).

Figure 40. Cover for French edition of *Nathalie Madoré*, 1895, color lithograph (cat. 36).

In addition to lithographic sheet music covers, posters, and the illustrations for the two books, *Le vagabond* and *La chanson des gueux*, Steinlen created 170 lithographs between 1889 and 1912 and a still undetermined number during World War I (cat. 89). The bulk of these, although initially produced in limited editions from 50 to 150, were subsequently printed in much larger editions, either to illustrate books—he made seventeen lithographs for *Les gueules noires*, 1907 (cat. 118)—or to be used as book covers for such works as, *Dans la rue* and *Nathalie Madoré* (fig. 40). Many of his other lithographs, as we have seen, were reproduced photomechanically either on the covers of *Le chambard*, 1893-94, and *La feuille*, 1898, or in the trade editions of *Chansons des femmes* and *Chansons de Montmartre*. The few exceptions to the mass printing or reproduction of his lithographs included *Dispute de filles*, 1895, in an edition of

Figure 41. *Frontal Portrait from the Waist Up of Maxim Gorki,* 1905,
        color lithograph (cat. 52).

fifty, and *Maxim Gorki,* 1905, a color lithograph
with only a few known proofs (fig. 41). In
addition, in 1896, Steinlen created *Coq et poules*
("Rooster and Hens") (cat. 41) and *Les chats*
("Cats") (fig. 42), two large lithographs printed
and published as part of Charles Verneau's
"L'estampe murale" series, which presented
items to be hung indoors as a decorative
alternative to posters.

The majority of Steinlen's commercial
work, whether sheet music covers, book
covers, or posters, used color as an essential
component.

Plate 7 . *In the Horse-drawn Coach,* ca. 1890, oil on canvas (cat. 221).

Figure 42. *Cats*, 1896, lithograph (cat. 42).

Figure 43. *Summer: Cat on a Balustrade*, 1909, color lithograph (cat. 53).

In contrast, his lithographic prints were primarily black and white. For some works, such as *Intérieur de tramway* ("Interior of a Streetcar"), which were in the stylistic and thematic tradition of Daumier, black and white may have been an aesthetic preference for Steinlen; but cost, too, must have been a factor. In 1909, Steinlen produced, in an edition of 250, two large striking color lithographs: *L'été: Chat sur une balustrade* ("Summer: Cat on a Balustrade") (fig. 43) and *L'hiver: Chat sur un coussin* ("Winter: Cat on a Cushion") (plate 8). During the war years, he created several other lithographs in color, such as *La gloire* ("Glory"), but again, black and white predominated (cat. 158). *La guerre* ("The War") was the title of two

Figure 44. *Forced March,* ca. 1916, lithograph (cat. 165).

series of black-and-white lithographs produced in 1916-17 (fig. 44). Together they consisted of more than thirty individual prints, each in an edition of one hundred, supplemented by larger editions of single lithographs depicting soldiers and civilians affected by the war (cat. 167).[9]

The most personal and also the most experimental of Steinlen's printed works were his etchings which he began in 1898, relatively late in his career, under the tutelage of the printer/artist Eugène Delâtre. Delâtre was the son of the great midcentury printer, Auguste Delâtre. By the early 1890s, Eugène was creating his own color etchings and by the end of the decade was revealing his technique to Louis Legrand, Auguste Lepère, Edgar Chahine, Steinlen, and even Picasso, among others.

9. For a discussion of this series see Camille Mauclair, "La guerre par Steinlen," *L'art et les artistes* (1918): pp. 3-40.

Figure 45. *Sketchbook page,* no date, ink (cat. 211).

Figure 46. *Laundresses Carrying Back Their Work*, 1898, color drypoint, aquatint, and line etching (cat. 1).

Emile Langlade, writer and friend of Delâtre, described the process in 1938:

> After having established a watercolor (design) with the three fundamental colors (yellow, red, blue), the artist makes a very detailed sketch on the copper in pure etching, sometimes recombs with dry point, and sometimes making use of aquatint and even softground. He uses this first plate for the printing of the darkest tone. Then he pulls a proof in black which he transfers to a smooth copper plate. On this new plate the second tone is etched, and so on, until the lightest tones are reached. He then proceeds to print the plates successively, beginning with the lightest tones.[10]

Steinlen produced 115 etchings between 1898 and 1912, more than a third of which were in color or a variety of grays and bistre. In 1913-14 he made a group of large softground nudes, depictions of cats by drypoint, and also by drypoint, Swiss landscapes in both color and black and white. Finally, during the war, he added a vigorous group of etchings and drypoints depicting war-related subjects. One of his last intaglio works was the 1922 drypoint which accompanied Antoine Parménie's *Autour de nos moulins* ("Around Our Windmills") (cat. 171). As with many of Steinlen's etchings, Eugène Delâtre did the printing and apparently liked it enough to use it as an address card.

Figure 47. *The Shower,* 1898, aquatint etching and drypoint (cat. 3).

10. Emile Langlade, *Artistes de mon temps,* (Arras: Editions I.N.S.A.P.,1938), pp. 11-27.

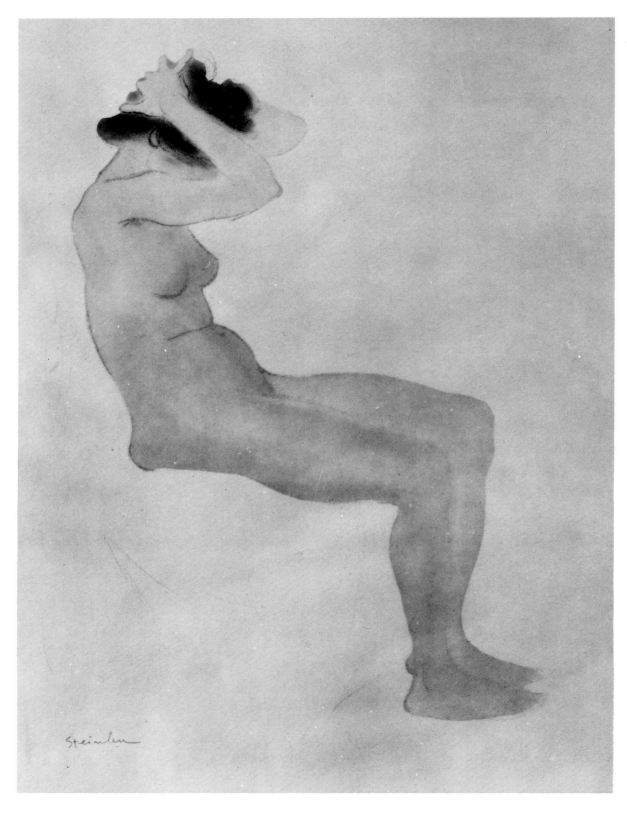

Figure 48. *Woman in Profile Combing Her Hair,* 1902, softground and aquatint etching (cat. 19).

The years 1898 and 1902 were by far Steinlen's most prolific in etching, with thirty-two prints in the first year and sixty-seven in 1902. His first four etchings were, in reality, experimental drypoint sketches or *croquis* limited to a maximum of ten proofs each. He scratched a variety of images onto zinc: nudes, portraits, and cats, scattering them helterskelter over the plate like many of his pen-and-pencil drawings (fig. 45). His experiments continued. He created prints in which drypoint lines combined with those produced by the bite of the acid and experimented with aquatint textures. In the spring of 1898, he printed, in editions of ten to thirty-two, several color etchings that employed many of the themes he had earlier used in magazine illustrations. Steinlen created a ghostly symbolic effect in *Fille et souteneur* ("Girl and Pimp") by making the figures emerge from the darkness of the rich aquatinted ground (plate 12). Working from dark to light, as in a mezzotint, by burnishing away the ink-receiving surface, he modeled and silhouetted the figures. Part of the eerie effect came from the suggestion of a glancing light reflecting off the two figures and their cat-like eyes. While this work and *La blanchisseuse* ("The Laundress") were each printed from one hand-colored plate, *Les Blanchisseuses reportant l'ouvrage* ("The

Figure 49. *The House on the Edge of Town,* 1902, color, softground, and aquatint etching (cat. 14).

Figure 50. *Cat on the Floor,* 1902, color drypoint, softground, and aquatint (cat. 18).

Laundresses Carrying Back Their Work")(fig. 46), with three plates, and *L'averse* ("The Shower")(fig. 47) and *Modèle lisant* ("Model Reading")(plate 9), each with two plates, followed Delâtre's more complicated instructions. In recognition of his debt to Delâtre, Steinlen inscribed the following dedication directly into one of the two plates used in the creation of the 1898 color drypoint, *Le petit chat* ("Little Cat") (C.27):

A l'ami Eug. Delâtre ce premier cuivre—résultat de ses bons conseils et de la gentillesse de son petit chat—est dédié. Juin 1898.

(To my friend Eug. Delâtre this first copper—result of his good counsel and the gentleness of his little cat—is dedicated. June 1898).

Plate 8. *Winter: Cat on a Cushion,*
1909, color lithograph
(cat. 54).

Plate 9. *Model Reading,* 1898,
color etching
(cat. 5).

65

Figure 51. *Quitting Time for Three Young Dressmakers,* 1900, color drypoint, (cat. 9).

In 1899, Steinlen used for the first time the technique of softground etching and combined it with aquatint in *Ménagère et enfants rentrant du lavoir* ("Housewife and Children Returning from the Laundry House"). 1902 found him intensely involved in etchings again, favoring the softground-aquatint combination in his ten simple and subtly textured female nude studies printed in bistre (fig. 48). During that year, he also combined softground and color with aquatint and drypoint in several quiet village landscapes and in numerous depictions of reclining cats (fig. 49, 50). In softground etching, Steinlen found an atmosphere and texture similar to his crayon and charcoal drawings (cat. 210).

Prior to the war, his etchings had no political content and rarely made social statements. Rather, they were often like his drawings, highly personal sketches and private inventions not created for a mass audience. Nudes, cats, and landscapes predominated as images of escape from the social-political arena of his other work, but his two types of works balanced each other rather than displacing each other. He did not desert his popular subjects and, furthermore, when the Society of One Hundred Bibliophiles commissioned him to produce etchings in large editions in 1900, he invariably chose a variation of his familiar street scenes (fig. 51).

Figure 52. *Belmont near Lausanne,* 1914, drypoint (cat. 150).

Figure 53. *Line of Five Soldiers*, ca. 1915, drypoint (cat. 155).

Figure 54. *The Liberator*, 1903, lithograph (cat. 51).

Steinlen's experiments in etching coincided with a period of creative activity in color etching at the turn of the century. In 1899, the Society of the Original Color Print had been founded with J.F. Rafaelli, whose own work, naturally, was dominated by color etching, as president. Steinlen, Manuel Robbe, the young Jacques Villon, and many others at the decade's end greatly enriched the vocabulary of color etching initiated by Raffaelli, Mary Cassatt, Eugène Delâtre, and Charles Maurin in the early 1890s. Steinlen's inventive use of the medium was one of his most important artistic accomplishments. His war etchings, however, were his final and ultimate innovation. Both in how he exploited the medium and in the universality of their statements, they demanded no less respect than that accorded to the work of Goya. Darkness and war were synonymous for Steinlen. In his war etchings and also in his wash lithographs of retreating and wounded soldiers, the darkness was relieved only by the flail of shells reflecting off barbed wire. His Swiss landscapes of 1913-14 had taught him the power of deeply scratched drypoint lines (fig. 52) and Steinlen now found that drypoint allowed him to suggest the horror and depersonalization of war most forcefully and dramatically (fig. 53).

Depersonalization—the despair and hopelessness of his anonymous faces—horrified Steinlen. That horror was a consistent theme in Steinlen's work in all media, whether the grinding force was poverty or war. In either case, Steinlen saw it as the greatest threat to justice and individual freedom. His optimistic art showed a just society raising the people from anonymity, and he portrayed that ideal—a socialist/republican society—allegorically by *La libératrice* ("The Liberator"), a bare-bosomed woman wearing a Phrygean cap (fig. 54); by an idealized woman symbolizing France, wearing a diaphanous cloak, a Phrygean cap, and a laurel wreath, and often carrying a shaft of wheat (fig. 55); by a

Figure 55. *Let's Stab Marianne,* no date, pastel (cat. 209).

Figure 56. *Homage to Zola,* ca. 1902, lithograph (cat. 148).

young female nude symbolizing truth (fig. 56); in his war etchings and lithographs by a flying woman carrying a sword, who represented France (fig. 57); and by a nurse, a symbol of national help (cat. 167).

The earliest depiction of this kind for Steinlen occurred in the mid-1880s with his painting of *Louise Michel sur les barricades* ("Louise Michel at the Barricades") (plate 5). Steinlen's work was based upon Eugène Delacroix's allegorical painting, *Liberty Leading the People,* 1830. Steinlen's painting, however, dealt with a particular individual and event: Louise Michel and the 18 March 1871 uprising of the Paris Commune in Montmartre. Significantly, the idealized Louise Michel, a political extremist, carried a red flag, the banner of the Commune, rather than the tricolor of the republic. Thus, she became the symbolic power of the Commune to liberate the proletariat from the oppression of the established order.

Figure 57. *The Mobilization*, 1915, etching (cat. 153).

Figure 58. *The First of May,* 1894, lithograph (cat. 29).

In 1894, Steinlen repeated this image with his lithograph and cover design entitled *Mai, 1871* ("May 1871") and for the socialist periodical *Le chambard.* However, the female figure was no longer identified as Louise Michel and instead was a generalized symbol of proletariat liberty. In another design for the same journal entitled *Le premier mai* ("The First of May"), an allegorical figure of Liberty led an immense international procession of workers (fig. 58), while in *Le 18 mars* ("March 18"), also for *Le chambard,* a similar figure led a procession of workers that included an artist (plate 7). As the decade of the 1890s progressed, Steinlen's Liberty sometimes protected and fed the poor (cat. 33), physically pulled the people from the depths of misery, freed them from their chains, and encouraged them to storm the bastion of oppression symbolized by the military and the church. Finally and predictably, during the war, Liberty became directly associated with the French Republic's struggle for military victory over Germany (fig. 59).

There is a direct correlation between Steinlen's depiction of women and his depiction of cats. He was an affectionate father to his only child, Colette, and seems to have been seriously involved with only two women—his wife and, after her death in 1910, his black mistress-model Massaida. His home was filled with cats to the point that 58, rue Caulaincourt during the early 1890s was nicknamed *Cat's Cottage.* The woman and the cat both seem to have symbolized a host of positive but sometimes conflicting qualities: strength, pride, grace, beauty, domesticity, and security. The defiant pose of Louise Michel or Liberty (plate 5, fig. 60) is quoted with an erect and

Figure 59. *The Republic Calls Us,* 1915,
       lithograph (cat. 156).

Figure 60. *May, 1871,* 1894,
       lithograph (cat. 31).

Figure 61. *The Black Cat Gaudeamus,* ca. 1890,
   oil on canvas (cat. 220).

aggressive cat in the painting, *Le chat noir
Gaudeamus* (fig. 61). His alley cats and
prostitutes both share a haughty independence
and alluring sensuousness (plate 18). In
contrast, his cats reposing on cushions, chairs,
etc. (plate 8) find domestic and seductive
parallels in his paintings, prints, and drawings
of reclining nudes (plate 9, fig. 62,63). His
parallel feline and female imagery helps
connect and harmonize the abundant variety of
subjects, themes, and media in Steinlen's art.
His humorous and light-hearted street people
are linked to his angry social-political
commentary, as his mass-produced illustrations
are linked to his limited editions by his
overriding empathy with human pain and his
joy in human potential.

Figure 62. *Seated Woman in Dressing Gown*, no date, charcoal and chalk (cat. 215).

Figure 63. *Reclining Nude*, no date, charcoal and chalk (cat. 216).

Plate 10. *The Trap,* 1900, color lithographic poster (cat. 86).

PHILLIP DENNIS CATE

II

Steinlen's Techniques for Photomechanical Illustration

In the 1880s, photomechanical processes took over the field of illustrating periodicals and books. Until 1878, all French publications had been illustrated by the traditional techniques of etching, wood or metal engraving, lithography, or by the relatively new process, gillotage.

Named after its inventor, Firmin Gillot, gillotage is a method of transforming an intaglio (etched) or planographic (lithographic) image into a relief image on a zinc plate for printing on a typographic press. By 1875, Charles Gillot, Firmin's son, had adapted his father's system to photography. In 1876, Charles set up the first photorelief print shop in Paris. By the end of that decade, Sarah Bernhardt's book *Dans les nuages* ("In the Clouds"), 1878, and the magazine *L'illustration*, 1879, inaugurated the era of relief photographic printing with their photomechanical illustrations taken from black line drawings.[1]

Many of the illustrations for *Le chat noir* magazine, including those by Steinlen, used this process which allowed no tonal values. For instance, creating *Les deux cochers* probably began by placing a photographic glass negative of the

simple black-and-white line drawing over a zinc plate covered with a ground of photo-sensitive bitumen (fig. 64). The negative and plate were exposed to light. The light hardened the exposed bitumen corresponding to the black line of the drawing and made it acid resistant. The bitumen not exposed to light was washed away; the plate was placed in acid which etched away the area between the lines, and the drawing appeared in relief ready to be inked and printed.

Photorelief printing had one disadvantage. Until the development of the half-tone screen in the mid-1880s, it could not reproduce shades, only lines. Artists soon learned how to manipulate the process, sometimes adding dots in their drawings to suggest tone, or by working directly on the relief plate to add what the film could not clearly produce. Charles Gillot also invented a variety of papers printed with rows of very fine striations of black lines or other consistent granular patterns. When an artist made his design on these papers, they would produce, during printing, values ranging from white to gray to black.

Steinlen used gillot paper for his illustration, *Amoureux* ("In Love"), which appeared in the 1888 volume of *Dans la rue* (fig. 65). The paper for this drawing was covered with a very fine pattern of black horizontal stripes. Using a pen and very dense black ink, Steinlen crisscrossed these stripes, producing the lines of the lamppost, windows, figures,

---

1. For more information on photoprinting and the artist in nineteenth-century France see Phillip Dennis Cate and Sinclair Hitchings, *The Color Revolution: Color Lithography in France 1890-1900*, (Salt Lake City: Peregrine Smith Inc., 1978).

Figure 64. *Les deux cochers*, 1886, pen and ink (cat. 175).

Figure 65. *In Love,* 1888, ink and blue crayon on Gillot paper (cat. 176).

and cart. He also scratched away the gillot stripes to make the white areas of the lights and the reflections in the street. In addition, a less dense group of lines was drawn over the gillot paper with a pencil, producing an intermediate value of gray. The man and the foreground street were drawn with black ink on an entirely different piece of plain white paper. Using a nonphotographic blue crayon, Steinlen then colored in areas of the arms, chest, legs, etc., indicating that he wanted an engraved mechanical pattern of dots to be later applied to these areas directly onto the zinc plate. These dots produced a fourth tonal pattern. Finally, the cut-out gillot paper design was glued behind the completed foreground figures and the entire image was ready to be photographed.

In the 1895 volume of *Dans la rue* Steinlen no longer used gillot paper for tonal effects but instead relied upon *crachis,* or the splattered ink technique used in his lithographic prints and posters since the early 1890s. *Crachis* rained irregular dots over the drawing, creating a tonal atmospheric effect. These often complicated but artistically creative systems of producing tonal drawings for photorelief-printed illustrations were gradually superseded toward the century's end with the relatively perfect half-tone screen.

Figure 66. *The Natural Pimp of Judges*, 1903, crayon (cat. 200).

Figure 67. Cover for *A Serious Customer*, 1897, stencil colored photorelief (cat. 106).

Unlike the black and white illustrations for *Le chat noir,* the 1888 cover design for *Dans la rue* and the illustrations for *Le mirliton* were stencil colored. For this process Steinlen took black and white proofs of the photorelief-printed illustrations and created watercolor models from which stencils, one for each color, would be made. This system often became quite complex, depending upon the number of stencils, but the covers of *Le chambard* and *La feuille,* as well as many of Steinlen's lithographic sheet music covers, used it (plate 11).

Although it was an inexpensive alternative to color lithographic printing, stencil coloring was not the only color system combined with photorelief-printed illustrations. The 1881 issue of *L'illustration* included photomechanical color illustrations for the first time in journalistic history. That same year the illustrations for *Imagerie artistique* including Steinlen's *Le portrait de Jules* were printed in color (cat. 145). Chromotypogravure or color photorelief printing was at this period a tedious and complicated task requiring the efforts of a technically skilled photographer and an engraver. The engraver produced one plate for each color to be used. Color separations could be made only by the sharp eye and the controlled hand of the engraver. Photomechanical color separation was purely experimental throughout the 1880s in the United States and France and had no practical application until the turn of the century.

The simplest color photorelief printing process required that a glass positive of a black linedrawing be placed over a zinc plate, previously prepared with a ground of photosensitive bitumen. All the areas of the drawing except those to be printed from that particular color plate were stopped out on the glass positive by an opaque pigment. The bitumen corresponding to the remaining drawing became hardened and acid-resistant when exposed to light. The unexposed bitumen, corresponding to the stopped-out areas of the drawing, was washed away, allowing acid to eat away the naked areas of the plate and placing the protected areas in relief, ready for printing on a letter press. This process allowed the printing of flat colors.

Mixing a granulated resin with the bitumen obtained more complicated printings. The printed color areas took on a speckled, aquatint quality which accommodated an intermixing of color and, since the white of the paper could show through, produced a lighter over-all effect. After all the complexities of the photo work were completed, it was still necessary to touch up each plate by hand before a successful color printing was possible. In producing color illustrations with any degree of creative artistic intent the engraver and the artist had to work together closely.

This was the system of color printing used in *Gil Blas illustré* (cat. 129-134), *Le rire, Le canard sauvage,* and *L'assiette au beurre.* Comparing the actual drawing with the final color printed illustration of *Le souteneur naturel des jugeurs* ("The Natural Pimp of the Judges") for the 14 November 1903 issue of *L'assiette au beurre* reveals that Steinlen drew this image first in black and white and even highlighted certain areas in white for sharper contrast in preparation (fig. 66). From this drawing, the photorelief plate was created. After this principal plate was made, he used the original drawing as the model for a red colorplate. Although Steinlen may have produced fully completed multi-color drawings as studies for his illustrations, it is clear that those actually photographed for reproduction in journals were not completed in color until the initial photorelief plate was made.

Photography allowed illustrations to be enlarged or reduced at will and to be printed over and over again. For Steinlen and other artists of the 1880s and 1890s, gillot paper and other tonal dot systems, as well as overseeing stencils and plates for color, were essential elements in the artistic exploitation and control of the medium of photoprinting (fig. 67).

Plate 11. *March 18,* 1894, stencil colored lithograph (cat. 24).

SUSAN GILL

III

Steinlen's Social and Political Imagery

Perhaps more than any other artist of his time, Théophile Alexandre Steinlen is remembered as an enemy of social injustice. As advocate for the poor, the downtrodden, and the working classes, Steinlen created images that mirrored a segment of French life—laundresses and errand girls, construction workers and miners, prostitutes and pimps—in the latter decades of the nineteenth century. Although his posters were often in a decorative style closely associated with Art Nouveau, most of his work grew out of the realist tradition of his masterful predecessors Gustave Courbet, Jean-François Millet, and Honoré Daumier.

His illustrations appeared in magazines linked to the leftist movement that emerged as a major political force in France in the 1890s, such as *Le chambard socialiste* and the anarchist publication *La feuille.* Yet these social commentaries grew out of his work illustrating popular literature.

The rising social awareness of the late nineteenth century produced a wave of poems, stories, novels, and even songs, in which social themes predominated.

The emergence of cafés and *café-concerts* provided a stage for songwriters with radical political beliefs who sympathetically portrayed the lower classes while ridiculing the rich. Steinlen's collaborator and first important influence was Aristide Bruant, whose *chansons*

réalistes dug deeper for their effects than other writers.[1] His subject was the underworld of prostitutes and pimps. His language was the rough and brutal argot of the streets. In the eleven years beginning in 1885 that Steinlen illustrated Bruant's *Le mirliton,* he created dozens of images of workers, wanderers, ragpickers, soldiers, the bourgeoisie, entertainers like Bruant and Yvette Guilbert, and, most frequently, the pitiable world of prostitution that dominated Bruant's verse (fig. 68).[2]

Steinlen was the key illustrator for *Gil Blas illustré* from 1891 through 1900, producing close to seven hundred images which the artistic community of Barcelona studied over the tables of Els Quatre Gats. The young Picasso was part of that circle.[3]

1. On Bruant, see Bettina Knapp, *Le Mirliton: A Novel Based on the Life of Aristide Bruant* (Paris: Nouvelles editions Debresse, 1969) which contains much documentary material on the singer; Oscar Méténier, *Aristide Bruant* (Paris: Au Mirliton, 1893); Arthur Symons, *Parisian Nights: A Book of Essays* (Westminster, England: The Beaumont Press, 1926), p. 13.

2. See my "Steinlen's Prints: Social Imagery in Late Nineteenth-Century Graphic Art," *The Print Collector's Newsletter,* 10, no. 1 (March-April 1979): 8-12.

3. See Marilyn McNully, *Els Quatre Gats: Art in Barcelona around 1900* (Princeton: Princeton University Press, 1978), p. 132; and Anthony Blunt and Phoebe Pool, *Picasso, The Formative Years: A Study of His Sources* (Paris: New York Graphic Society, 1962.

Figure 68. *Aristide Bruant,* 1895, crayon (cat. 188).

Gil Blas illustré was a highly influential weekly literary supplement to the daily newspaper, *Gil Blas.* The German *Simplicissimus,* to which Steinlen also contributed at least one illustration, was established as its counterpart.[4] The contents were diverse, but included contributions from a group primarily concerned with depicting the lower classes in an extension of the naturalistic school of the Goncourts and Emile Zola (fig. 69). This group included Zola himself, Bruant, de Maupassant, Richepin, Jehan Rictus, and Camille de Saint-Croix and produced novels, stories, poems, and songs (cat. 194,195).

Steinlen usually illustrated a specific incident from a story in his contributions to *Gil Blas illustré.* In so doing, he created a record of his day's social concerns. Among the characters he captured were the *trottin* ("errand girl"), the *midinette* ("Parisian dressmaker"), vagabonds, homeless children, and, most compelling, his prostitutes (fig. 70, plate 18). With a minimum of detail, his creations came alive with the harsh expressions and candid gestures of the street.

Elements of symbolism may be found in Steinlen's stark depictions. For example, in *Les marcheuses* ("The Streetwalkers"), 1893, an illustration for a Bruant song, the coarse face and desperate movement of the woman in the foreground are highly realistic, but the background figures, drawn more abstractly, take on the mystery and ambiguity of symbolism (fig. 70). They are derived from an illustration of the same song published a month earlier in *Le mirliton* in which five figures dressed in black appear to glide through the night. The rhythmic, abstract pattern of their dark silhouettes achieves an effect similar to that aimed at by symbolist works of the period and is also subtly sensitive to Bruant's verse.

Figure 69. *End of the Idyll,* 1895, pastel (cat. 91).

4. Stanley Applebaum, *Simplicissimus* (New York: Dover Publications, Inc., 1975), p. ix.

Figure 70. *The Street Walkers,* cover illustration for *Gil Blas illustré,* photorelief.
Courtesy Mr. and Mrs. Herbert D. Schimmel.

The song's twelve stanzas have a sense of rhythm and movement unusual for Bruant, largely because of the repetition of a singular refrain six times:

> Pierreuses, trotteuses,
> A's marchant l'soir
> Quand il fait noir,
> Sur le trottoir.

> (Prostitutes, streetwalkers,
> Parade in the evening darkness
> On the sidewalk.)

Three years later, Steinlen recreated the feeling of Les marcheuses in another striking illustration of prostitutes, the highly expressive Ballade d'hiver ("Winter Ballad"), illustrating a short piece by Gustave Coquiot (fig. 71). These figures made their way through the stark darkness, shivering in the glare of electric lights amid the bare trees of winter. In such works, Steinlen used lines to suggest the rhythms of poetry and music, and he relied upon his pictoral structure to create a mood of alienation and melancholy, much as his contemporary Edvard Munch used color and line to evoke the spiritual turbulence of modern existence.

Steinlen's illustrations of the city vagrants were also among his most powerful in Gil Blas illustré. It was not surprising that stories about these types were written, since between 1830 and 1890 the number of reported vagabonds and beggars rose from 2,500 to 20,000. In 1899, 50,000 of them were arrested.[5] In 1907, a Commission du vagabondage was named in the Chamber of Deputies to deal with the problem. In Gil Blas illustré the vagabond appeared as a victim of industrialism's unemployment and displacement, usually with sympathetic attention to the psychology underlying his way of life and the social conditions to which he was subjected. Some stories attacked the inequities of the class structure, showing the vagabond's violent actions springing from a desire to redress these inequities.

For L'homme des berges ("The Barge Man") by Jean Lorrain, the story of a ruthless mugger, Steinlen set his figure against the Seine and the island of the Grand Jatte, a desolate landscape from which all life has vanished (fig. 72). By showing him in a light-colored smock—the worker's blouse suaire—Steinlen focused attention on the vagrant's face and evoked a menacing quality by the stooped shoulders, hidden hands, and wild stare of this figure.

Another moving portrayal of a city prowler is Le vilain homme ("The Wretched Man"), a drawing for a Gil Blas story by Lucien Descaves, published 19 November 1897 (fig. 73). The principal character, a social rebel, deliberately frightens people by peering through restaurant windows while they are eating. This vagrant ascribes his behavior to quasi-political reasons:

> On ne me plaint pas, cependant; je ne veux pas qu'on me plaigne; il est trop facile de plaindre les pauvres quand on a chaud et qu'on a bien dîné. Mieux vaut inspirer la terreur que la compassion: la terreur réconforte davantage celui qui la répand. On voit tout de suite que je ne mendie pas, on le voit dans mes yeux étincelants et sur ma lèvre amère; leur expression est pire que l'outrage et met le désordre dans les âmes!

> (No one pities me, however, I don't want anyone to pity me; it is too easy to pity the poor when you're warm and have just eaten a good dinner. Better to inspire terror than compassion; terror is more comforting to the one who spreads it. You can see right away that I'm not begging; you see it in my glaring eyes and my bitter lips. Their expression is worse than outrage and spreads disorder in souls.)

Later he describes his attitude as that of someone who demands from people, "Tout ou Rien" ("All or Nothing"). Steinlen shows the

5. Fernande Dubief, La question du vagabondage (Paris: Charpentier, 1911), p. 20.

6ᵉ ANNÉE. — N° 11 *

13 MARS 1896

RÉDACTION ET ADMINISTRATION
8, rue Glück, Paris

RÉCLAMES : 10 fr. la ligne
ANNONCES : 5 fr. la ligne

RENÉ MAIZEROY
DIRECTEUR

Prix de l'abonnement au *Gil Blas* quotidien
3 mois : Paris, 13 fr 50. Départ. 16 fr.
Prix du Numéro : PARIS, 15 c. PROVINCE. 20 c.

ABONNEMENTS

France Étrang.
Trois mois .... 1 fr.   2 fr.
Six mois .... 2 fr.   4 fr.
Un an .... 4 fr.   8 fr.

Le **GIL BLAS** illustré est servi
en prime à tous les abonnés du
GIL BLAS quotidien

Journal littéraire, politique et mondain

3 mois : Paris, 13 fr 50. Départ 16 fr.
Prix du Numéro : PARIS, 15 c., PROVINCE. 20 c.

GIL BLAS

ILLUSTRÉ, HEBDOMADAIRE

*Amuser les gens qui passent, leur plaire aujourd'hui et recommencer
le lendemain.* — J. JANIN, préface de Gil Blas

BALLADE D'HIVER, par Gustave Coquiot

(Dessin de Steinlen.)

Figure 71. *Winter Ballad,* cover illustration for *Gil Blas illustré,* 13 March 1896, color photorelief.
Courtesy Mr. and Mrs. Herbert D. Schimmel.

vagrant staring malevolently through a restaurant at a fat bourgeois man while he is eating. A well-dressed couple in the background further stresses the social divisions against which this ominous figure is rebelling.

In 1893, using the pseudonym *Petit Pierre*, Steinlen began contributing to the Marxist periodical, *Le chambard socialiste*, established in response to the growing struggle between the government and the Left during the 1890s—a struggle that was itself prompted by violent anarchist demonstrations. Its first number appeared one week after Auguste Vaillant threw a bomb onto the floor of the Chamber of Deputies, generating repressive measures against socialism. The magazine proposed to act as an arm of the socialist parties, to represent all leftist organizations, and to defend the exploited and unfortunate members of the social order. It claimed that it would denounce *"sans peur ni merci, les iniquités sociales et leurs auteurs, les exactions des exploitants, les canailleries et les corruptions gouvernmentales"*[6] ("without fear or mercy, social inequities and their authors, the exactions of exploiters, the dirty tricks and corruptions of the government").

From its very first issue, *Le chambard* was successful beyond all expectations and the printer's supply was quickly exhausted. Steinlen's large-scale, full-page, colored covers, measuring approximately 12 7/8 by 7 1/4 inches, must have helped attract the public to this inexpensive weekly, which sold for ten centimes. Shortly after the newspaper was first published, it announced that covers could be purchased as original numbered lithographs through the printer E. Kleinmann.[7] Kleinmann printed one hundred lithographs of each cover illustration on high-grade white paper, and in some cases, pulled additional prints on a cheaper yellow paper.

Figure 72. *The Barge Man,* cover illustration for *Gil Blas illustré,* 22 March 1896, color photorelief.
Courtesy Mr. and Mrs. Herbert D. Schimmel.

6. *Le chambard socialiste* no. 1, 16 Dec. 1893, p. 4.

7. Kleinmann followed this procedure for all but one cover, *Le jeune ministre*, no. 26, 9 June 1894, for which the stone was damaged. See Ernest de Crauzat, *L'ouevre gravée et lithographiée de Steinlen* (Paris: Société de propagation des livres d'art, 1913), pp. 196-97.

Figure 73. *The Wretched Man*, cover illustration for *Gil Blas illustré*, 19 November 1897, color photorelief. Courtesy Mr. and Mrs. Herbert D. Schimmel.

Two popular covers, *Adjourd'hui* ("Today") and *Demain* ("Tomorrow"), appeared on the two consecutive issues of March and April 1894 and accurately represented its editorial position (fig. 74,75). The first showed the capitalist as a tyrannical slavedriver, treating his workers like animals. In the second, the worker had literally broken the yoke of oppression and was master of his own destiny.

Steinlen's businessman in these images was stereotypical of the 1890s: corpulent, smoking a cigar, and having a large nose. This stereotype often had anti-Semitic overtones when Jews and oppressive capitalism were equated.

Gérault-Richard's editorials in *Le chambard* linked big business and government as oppressors of the people, an idea vividly captured by two of Steinlen's illustrations. In *Cent millions!* ("One Hundred Million!"), 1894, two soldiers were seen saluting a businessman as though he were a military official. The caption read: *M. le Baron est mis en liberté avec les honneurs dûs à un personnage de haut vol* ("Monsieur the Baron is released from prison with all the honors due a personage of grand larceny"). Gérault-Richard, in the previous issue of *Le chambard,* had denounced one of the ministers for having stated that *"Le drapeau rouge est le drapeau de l'armée du vol"* ("The red flag is the flag of the thieves army"). The socialists, he continued, were accused of dishonesty by the government, but it was the ministers who were the thieves. He named, in particular, those involved in the Panama scandal.[8]

It was a notable attack. A French company had been established in 1881 to dig the Panama Canal—an ambitious, but ultimately unsuccessful, project that had attracted enormous public investments. In 1893, the directors of the Panama Canal Company and several deputies had been brought to trial. The deputies were accused of accepting bribes from company members to support a lottery-loan eventually issued by the government to the sinking company. Except for one deputy who confessed, all parties were acquitted—a fact that the leftists viewed with great bitterness.

In his *Cent millions!,* Steinlen depicted the capitalists as thieves who had deceived the people into investing hundreds of millions of francs in a doomed company. The cover went well beyond the editorial, incorporating details that succinctly summarized the Panama affair. For example, the caption alluded to a baron who was given his liberty, most probably Baron Jacques de Reinach, an agent of the Panama Canal Company and a key figure in the scheme to bribe the Chamber. Reinach had committed suicide two years before this illustration, certain that he would be exposed for his involvement in the scandal. To Steinlen, Reinach symbolized the corruption uncovered by the scandal. Even though the baron had, in fact, already died, in the illustration he is being given his liberty, like those on trial in 1893. By weaving together the public's memory of the baron and his suicide—which touched off a public outcry for a complete and thorough inquiry—with the more recent event of the

8. "Instruisons-nous," *Le chambard socialiste,* 17 February 1894, p. 2.

Figure 74. *Today!,* 1894, stencil colored lithograph (cat. 26).

Figure 75. *Tomorrow!*, 1894, stencil colored lithograph (cat. 27).

acquittal, Steinlen created an extremely provocative image of the scandal.

Even without understanding the specific allusions in *Cent millions!*, the cover is readily understandable. A second cover illustrating the partnership of business and government on 19 May 1894 is more elusive (fig. 76). Its caption reads: *Dans les conflits entre patrons et ouvriers la place du la législature est du côté de la caisse et non parmi les grévistes (La majorité opportuniste)* ("In conflicts between bosses and workers the legislature's

Figure 76. *The Opportunist Majority,* 1894, lithograph (cat. 30).

place is on the side of the money, not among the strikers (the opportunistic majority)"). The satire of this cover depends heavily on its caption. Are these two men both capitalists collecting their dividends? One is, but is the other man slipping something into his pocket another industrialist, or, rather, a government official?

Gérault-Richard's editorial gave no indication of this man's identity. However, an editorial in the previous issue named several individuals who sided with the owners against the workers at the mines of Anzin, including the Minister of Finance, Maurice Rouvier, who had been indicted in the Panama scandal but cleared of all charges because of a legal technicality. The drawing may have alluded to him—a highly placed government official sharing the businessman's profits—or it may have been a deliberately ambiguous illustration of Gérault-Richard's numerous assertions of corruption and thievery in the government.

If the businessman was the villain of *Le chambard*, Liberty, the personification of the Republic, was its heroine. She appeared frequently in its pages, sometimes being abducted by the businessman. Perhaps Steinlen's most successful portrayal of this allegorical figure was his illustration commemorating the day *Le 18 mars*, when the people of Paris seized the weapons of the regular army in 1871 (plate 11). Steinlen showed Liberty marching triumphant at the head of an army of workers, flanked on her right by a miner and a farmer, and on her left by a factory worker, or artisan, and an artist. In the background, a lively frieze of flying arms, pitchforks, axes, and spades symbolized the multitude of workers who had joined together to fight the enemies of the Republic.[9]

The image and spirit of the Commune was an important symbol to the socialists in the 1890s. In addition to *Le 18 mars*, Steinlen used this event for several more illustrations in *Le chambard*. Two of his most forceful were *Le cri des pavés!* ("The Scream of the Pavement!") (fig. 77) and *Au mur des Fédérés* ("At the Wall of the Federationists"), in which his gory visions approached the spirit of Goya's *Disasters of War*. *Le cri des pavés* represented "Bloody Week" in

Figure 77. *The Scream of the Pavement!* 1894, stencil colored lithograph (cat. 23).

9. A drawing for *Le 18 mars* in the Musée municipal d'art et d'histoire, St. Denis, contains a figure at the left in a dark top hat that seems to have been drawn from Delacroix's *Liberty Leading the People*, a work Steinlen could have seen in the Louvre. An undated painting by Steinlen in the Louvre, *Jeune femme assise sur un canapé*, is a freely drawn copy of Delacroix's *Chevaux arabes se battant dans une écurie* ("Arab Horses Fighting in a Stable"). Linda Nochlin has further pointed out the influence of one of Delacroix's Faust lithographs, *Marguerite and Faust in Prison*, on Steinlen's *La famine*, 1922 (B.N. Inventaire RF 31785).

May 1871, when the Communards were repressed, and between twenty and twenty-five thousand of them died. Steinlen showed the cadaverous figures screaming for help and lifting futile arms as they drowned in a sea of blood. The red flag had fallen from the hand of one. In *Au mur des Fédérés*, the Communards were seen rising from the dead at the famous wall in Père-Lachaise cemetery where many of them had died fighting. The wall was covered with wreaths, commonly placed there on May Day in remembrance of the dead.

Steinlen's illustrations for *Le chambard* represented a stylistic departure from the painterly, atmospheric technique perfected in *Gil Blas illustré*. For the didactic socialist periodical, he created obvious stereotypes and allegorical figures drawn with crisp outlines and occasional patches of color. This style represented Steinlen's commitment to reach a working class readership clearly. While the images may have appeared crude and over-simplified, they were very effective propaganda for the working-class audience, imitated as such by subsequent contributors.

In 1897, the prolific Steinlen became the chief contributor to another political periodical, the anarchist *La feuille*, which ran from 1897 through 1899. Its editor-in-chief and only writer was Zo d'Axa, a pen name for Charles Galland. The collaboration was immensely fruitful (fig. 78). Gérault-Richard was basically a politico who wrote, but d'Axa was primarily a writer with political interests. While *Le chambard*

with its dogmatic propaganda appealed successfully to the lower classes, *La feuille* was more sophisticated, aimed at an intellectual group, and was anything but didactic. In fact, d'Axa refused association with any political party and specifically denied that he was an anarchist, even though he had edited a celebrated anarchist newspaper, *L'en dehors* ("The Outsider"), published May 1891-January 1893. In his definition of the *en dehors* person, d'Axa summarized the spirit he would breathe into *La feuille* as well:

> *Celui qui rien n'enrôle et qu'une impulsive nature guide seule, ce passionnel tant complexe, ce hors-la-loi, ce hors d'école, cet isolé, chercheur d'au-delá . . .* [10]

(He who nothing conscripts and who is guided only by his impulsive nature and the complexities of his passions, this outlaw, outside of any school, this isolated one, this seeker of the beyond . . .)

This sense of political independence characterized Steinlen as well. Although he lent his services to political publications, he never joined a political party.

The articles in *La feuille* did not report political events, but provided a satirical commentary unique to Zo d'Axa, who had a gift for linking several seemingly unrelated political and social problems within one article. Steinlen's illustrations responded with subtlety and skill to the violence, wit, and irony of d'Axa's texts.

10. As cited in Jean Maitron, *Le mouvement anarchiste en France*, (Paris: Librarie François Maspero, 1975), 1: 37.

Figure 78. Cover for *From Mazas to Jerusalem*, 1895, stencil colored photorelief (cat. 105).

Figure 79. *The Franco-Russian Payment*, 1897,
lithograph (cat. 44).

For example, d'Axa's first editorial for *La feuille*, October 1897, took as its subject the Franco-Russian Alliance (fig. 79). Since the early 1890s a loose alliance between France and Russia had consisted of the understanding that France would help Russia financially and militarily and that Russia would reciprocate with military aid against the Triple Alliance of Germany, Austria-Hungary, and Italy. The agreement had been made secretly in the mid-1890s, but President Félix Faure officially acknowledged it in August 1897 during a trip to Russia. The alliance was much criticized, particularly by leftists who found it reprehensible that France would lend large sums of money to Russia when her own people were in need. Moreover, the Tsar's dictatorship was anathema to leftists of all persuasions.

In d'Axa's *"La première aux propriétaires"* ("The First One for the Landlords"), he set up a fictional situation—a device he often used—which called ironic attention to the repercussions of the alliance. In a celebration of the Franco-Russian Alliance, he showed French landlords allowing tenants rent-free periods in honor of Russian protection, then admitted it was "too much to ask," and launched a bitter attack, claiming that an alliance aided the landlords at the expense of the poor.

Steinlen's illustration matched the violent tone. *Le terme Franco-Russe* ("The French-Russian Payment"), which was also d'Axa's subtitle, depicted a poor family watching with bowed heads as a fierce policeman supervised their eviction and their possessions were carted off. In the foreground, a child played innocently with toy flags of France and Russia. This was hardly the fictional *terme* or three-month grace period for tenants d'Axa proposed but rather its denial. Steinlen's illustration was the brutal literalization of d'Axa's satire. Furthermore, d'Axa had discussed the exploitation of the poor in general terms and specifically mentioned tramps and children being sent to abusive correctional institutions, but the idea of an eviction was Steinlen's own contribution, an effective illustration of the fact underlying d'Axa's sentiment and the creation of a second satire on the Franco-Russian Alliance.

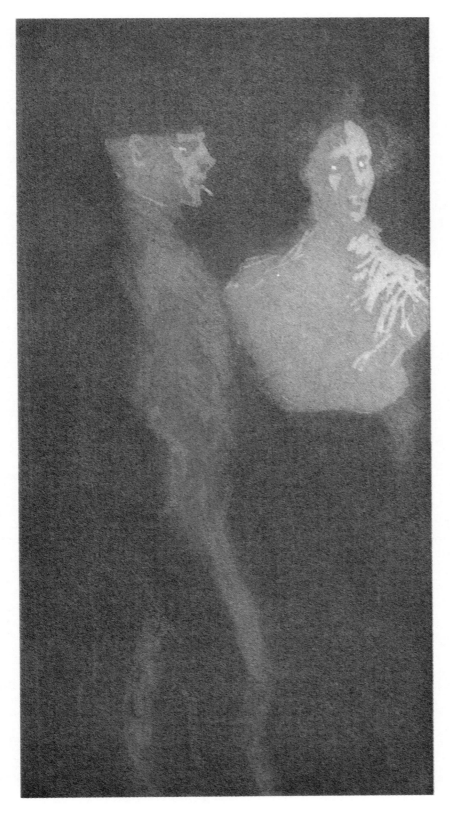

Plate 12. *Girl and Pimp*, 1898, color aquatint (cat. 2).

Steinlen usually used either the title or subtitle of d'Axa's article as a point of departure for his illustration. The harmony of work indicates the personal relation between the men. Another clue lies in numerous drawings Steinlen made of d'Axa, a testament to his admiration and affection for the writer.[11]

In addition to the Franco-Russian Alliance, d'Axa also dealt memorably with such issues as disarmament, the role of journalists, the mistreatment of young soldiers, and the repression of poor urban youths. However, the Dreyfus affair, which erupted in 1897, focused his energies and became *La feuille's* supreme cause. Steinlen's illustrations of this episode, comparable in our own time to Watergate, graphically chronicled this historic struggle for justice.

In 1894, a French agent had discovered a *bordereau* ("memorandum") in a wastebasket at the German Embassy in Paris and took it to the counterespionage department of the French General Staff. The *bordereau,* addressed to the German military attaché, indicated that an officer within the French War Ministry— probably attached to the General Staff—was supplying the Germans with military secrets. Alfred Dreyfus, a Jewish officer, was singled out, tried, and condemned to solitary confinement on Devil's Island, although he insisted he was innocent and there was virtually no conclusive evidence against him. As one of the few Jews in the officer corps during a period in which anti-Semitism in France was on the rise, he was an obvious scapegoat.

Public attention gradually became intense and the Dreyfus affair soon became the battleground between conservative nationalists and the liberal republicans, who called for a review of the case. The battle took several years. But in 1899, Dreyfus was called back

from Devil's Island, fully vindicated by a civilian court in 1906, and reinstated as a lieutenant in the army.

Most radicals initially reacted to the Dreyfus affair with scornful indifference. Why, leftist journalists queried, was so much space being devoted to the troubles of a rich officer while the grave social problems of France went ignored? However, as the case developed, many radicals recognized that the fundamental individual rights on which the Republic was based were at stake. Eventually, a "revolutionary coalition" of anarchists and socialists was established to support Dreyfus.

Steinlen's attitude toward the Dreyfus affair also seems to have evolved with new developments. Although ambivalent before the Dreyfus case, a study of his *La feuille* illustrations reveals that, like Zo d'Axa and many other radicals, he became more involved as the case progressed. His involvement grew to such an extent that in 1899 he signed a petition with other artists and literary figures in support of Colonel Georges Picquart, who had been courtmartialed for his support of Dreyfus.[12]

D'Axa's *"Association de malfaiteurs"* ("Association of Wrongdoers"), published in late November 1897, expressed his disgust at the rumors of plots and counterplots, of papers stolen, documents suppressed, and wrongdoing concealed. He called on the president and the army to set the record straight and break the

11. On Steinlen's friendship with Zo d'Axa see Georges Auriol, *Steinlen et la rue* (Paris: E. Rey, 1930), pp. 15ff. Steinlen made numerous drawings of men he admired, including Anatole France, Maxim Gorki, and Zo d'Axa.

12. Robert Byrnes, *Antisemitism in Modern France* (New Brunswick: Rutgers University Press, 1950), p. 291, includes Steinlen in a list of anti-Semitic artists. Alexander Seltzer maintains that Steinlen was neutral on the issue in his "Anarchism, Antisemitism and the Press: A Critical Evaluation of Three Artists' Response to the Dreyfus Affair" (Thesis, University of Cincinnati, 1972). Eugenia W. Herbert includes Steinlen in a list of radicals who were for revision, *The Artist and Social Reform: France and Belgium, 1885-1895* (New York: Books for Libraries Press, 1961), p. 202. Marguerite Steinlen, the artist's niece, who lived with Steinlen in Paris prior to his death, claims that Steinlen fought for revision. See "Steinlen," *Du,* May 1953, p. 31. Paul Brenet and Félix Thureau, *Hommage des artistes à Picquart* (Paris: Société libre d'édition des gens de lettres, 1899), p. 103.

Plate 13. *The Mad People,* drawing for cover illustration of *Gil Blas illustré,* 15 December 1895, watercolor and ink (cat. 189).

Figure 80. *Striking Arguments,* cover illustration for *La Feuille,* 21 January 1898, photorelief. Courtesy Mr. and Mrs. Herbert D. Schimmel.

web of complicity at the top echelons of government. Sarcastically he exclaimed *"En vérité, j'écris: ce n'est pas nous qui sommes une Association de malfaiteurs!"* ("In truth, I write: it is not we who are an association of wrongdoers!"), a quotation from the repressive laws against anarchists passed in 1893. One of these laws redefined *"association de malfaiteurs"* to include anarchists who perpetrated violent acts or even those who knew about or intended such acts. These laws resulted in the dissolution of several left-wing journals, including *L'en dehors* and the arrest of many editors and writers, including d'Axa.

Steinlen's illustration of this article did not show any great commitment. Titled *Association de malfaiteurs*, it showed not criminals, but well-to-do members of the bourgeoisie, huddled together conspiratorially, in shiny top hats and greatcoats. The atmosphere of intrigue was thus captured, but where d'Axa wrote about Army officers, Steinlen included only one soldier, almost hidden, in the back. The rest were businessmen, government officials, or members of the middle- and upperclasses. Thus Steinlen avoided an open accusation of the army, a fair position at a time when information about the Dreyfus case was at best confused and incomplete.

The attitude of both Zo d'Axa and Steinlen toward the Dreyfus affair became more emphatic after Zola's famous *"J'accuse"* ("I Accuse"), published in *L'Aurore* on 13 January 1898, flung down the gauntlet to political and military leaders. The article created a furor. Zola was arrested and tried for libel. Anti-Semitism erupted. In many French cities, mobs beat Jews and plundered their shops. Students stormed Zola's house, shouting "Death to Zola! Long live the Army!" But Zola had rallied the Left.

On 21 January, just one week after *"J'accuse,"* d'Axa forcefully endorsed the revision of the Dreyfus case with *Arguments frappants* ("Striking Arguments"), a bitter pun (fig. 80). Focusing on the mob violence that followed Zola's article, he cited three specific acts of brutality against innocent workers, including one incident where three soldiers beat a laborer to death. D'Axa denounced the injustices of a system in which privates could be executed for misconduct—the subject of a previous editorial—yet given light sentences for killing a civilian. He further attacked the prejudiced military judges who acquitted Commandant Ferdinand Walsin Esterhazy, the true author of the *bordereau*, and called for a complete investigation. Of the three incidents that d'Axa cited, one involved a Jew, and d'Axa saw him as representative of an individual defenseless in the face of injustice and mob violence:

> *C'est toujours la même aventure: dès qu'un pauvre diable est sans défense, il y a des braves qui se révèlent. Dans les bagarres, quand on trébuche, les talons de bottes frappent à la tête. Essayer d'arracher aux foules une des victimes de leur lynchage déchaîne des colères de bêtes auxquelles on enlève la proie.*

> (It's always the same story: as soon as a poor devil is defenseless, some brave bullies show themselves. In brawls, as soon as you falter, bootheels kick you in the head. Try to snatch a lynch victim from the crowd and you unleash the wrath of beasts from whom you take their prey.)

Steinlen brilliantly portrayed the mob's anger in his illustration *Arguments frappants*. Using the vertical format of the newspaper, Steinlen placed a fallen man at the very bottom of the page, surrounded by a jeering crowd descending upon him. One man kicked him in the shoulder and another brought a stick down on him. As in d'Axa's article, the helpless man was Dreyfus, the victim of humanity gone mad. At this point, Steinlen had taken a stand.[13]

13. Ralph E. Shikes, *The Indignant Eye* (Boston: Beacon Press, 1969), pp. 229-30, also interprets this illustration as an allegory of the Dreyfus case.

Two other Steinlen illustrations revealed his sympathy with Dreyfus and his hostility toward the nationalist factions. On 28 February 1898, days after Zola was condemned for libel, d'Axa published *Les moutons de Boisdeffre* ("Boisdeffre's Sheep"). Boisdeffre was the chief of the General Staff, and Zola had accused him of concealing evidence in the Dreyfus case. D'Axa condemned the army as an enemy of liberty and hence of the Republic, reproached the mob's blind allegiance to the military, and warned against the dangerous alliance between the Church and the army, which the affair had strengthened.

As in *Arguments frappants*, Steinlen focused on the mob in *Les moutons de Boisdeffre* (fig. 81). The second composition drew on the first with the repeated image of a dense crowd of people with dramatically animated facial expressions and gestures. It was Steinlen's only repetition in *La feuille*, indicating that he felt that his hysterical mobs effectively captured one of the most characteristic aspects of the affair.

In both illustrations, he represented the mob realistically, but in *Les moutons* he introduced a symbol, a sword which a detached hand thrust into the crowd. The situation was thus not literal. The sword was a contemporary allusion to the army but it also quoted d'Axa's condemnation in the previous issue of *La feuille* of *"la justice de sabre!"* Moreover, Jean Jaurès, a socialist deputy whom Steinlen greatly admired, had spoken in the Chamber of the "tyranny of the sword," explaining the sympathy of the socialists toward Dreyfus. The figures in this illustration cheered the sword but simultaneously cowered from it in fear. Several social classes were represented, but the most dominant were a soldier and a clergyman, the clergyman resting his hand amicably on the back of the soldier. By now Steinlen's antimilitarism could not be overlooked; and since a criticism of the army was an expression of sympathy to Dreyfus, Steinlen was being deliberately provocative.

Steinlen's antimilitaristic and anticlerical attitude was further expressed in an illustration which accompanied d'Axa's *Rochefort se meurt! Rochefort est mort!* ("Rochefort is dying!

Rochefort is dead!"), which appeared on 16 June 1898. Steinlen showed the body of Henri Rochefort, a political journalist, being carried away from a funeral service (fig. 82). Actually, Rochefort would not die until 1913, but d'Axa, his bitter opponent, was claiming his spiritual death. Rochefort was not actually a Communard in 1871, but his approval of it had resulted in imprisonment and exile to New Caledonia until amnesty was declared in 1880. Rochefort then returned to Paris and became an archconservative, writing virulent articles against Dreyfus, and for the military, in his newspaper *L'intransigeant* ("The Intransigent").

D'Axa accused Rochefort of opportunism—of exploiting aspects of the Dreyfus affair to raise his circulation—and poured contempt on Rochefort's defense of militarism:

> *Le militarisme est la clef de voûte du monument d'iniquité, de misère, de laideur, d'exploitation que représente cette société. Le soldat est le chien de garde des receleurs capitalistes—et c'est le chien de fusil des grèves. . . . Marcher avec la soldatesque n'est pas l'acte d'un insurgé; mais c'est le fait d'une bonne d'enfant: Rochefort est une nourrice sèche pour troupiers de l'état-major.*

> (Militarism is the keystone of the monument of iniquity, misery, ugliness, and exploitation that this society represents. The soldier is the watchdog for the capitalist fence, the trigger for strikes. . . . To march with the soldiery is not the act of an insurgent, but the deed of a nursemaid. Rochefort is a wetnurse gone dry for the troops of the chief of staff.)

Figure 81. *Boisdeffre's Sheep,* cover illustration for *La Feuille,* 28 February 1898, photorelief. Courtesy Mr. and Mrs. Herbert D. Schimmel.

Figure 82. *Rochefort is Dying! Rochefort is Dead,* cover illustration for *La feuille,* 16 June 1898, photorelief. Courtesy Mr. and Mrs. Herbert D. Schimmel.

Figure 83. *Ten Assassinations for a Penny*, 1897, lithograph (cat. 45).

In Steinlen's pro-Dreyfus illustration, the writer was being honored by several groups, most prominently army officers, some of whom may have caricatured specific officers. This satirical representation also included in the background a bishop surrounded by choirboys and a priest who blessed the body. Steinlen's association of anticlericalism and antimilitarism was far more trenchant even than d'Axa's astringent text. At this point, Steinlen, like his friends Zo d'Axa, Gérault-Richard, Jean Jaurès, and Anatole France, to name but a few, was clearly a confirmed Dreyfusard.

Stylistically, Steinlen's illustrations for *La feuille* represent a different spirit from those he had created for *Gil Blas illustré* and *Le chambard socialiste*. A sense of gloom and violence that paralleled the pessimism of Zo d'Axa permeate his sombre images. Marked by strong contrasts of black and white, they have an unsettling, even a frightening, quality (fig. 83). Like the texts they illustrate, they are designed to shock the reader and enlist him against deep-seated problems in French society. Again, Steinlen's remarkable ability to adapt his style to the demands made by diverse periodicals is striking. His versatility as an illustrator sets him above the great majority of his contemporaries, as does his commitment to humanitarian ideals.

Plate 14. *White Slavery*, 1899, color lithographic poster (cat. 82).

SUSAN GILL

IV

Steinlen's Posters: Aesthetics and Influence

Steinlen's posters were an important development in his career as an illustrator. During the 1880s and early 1890s, his work as a magazine illustrator gave him a solid reputation; but with the posters he produced during the mid-and late 1890s, he was celebrated, along with Chéret, Eugène Grasset, Alphonse Mucha, and Toulouse-Lautrec, as one of the leaders in French poster art of his time.

The poster movement, which dominated the graphic arts of the 1890s, coincided with a decorative arts revival that began in France about 1889 and lasted until the 1920s. The poster revival has attracted a great deal of critical attention, but little has been said of the French decorative arts revival despite the reciprocity of the two movements.[1]

This *fin-de-siècle* revival had begun with the Great Exhibition of 1851 in London. Léon de Laborde, an art historian and critic, was officially commissioned to report on the applied arts, and like William Morris and Owen Jones, was appalled by the inferior quality of so many of the objects exhibited. Candidly, he expressed his dismay at the French section, replete with lifeless imitation of Empire styles. The experience made Laborde a crusader for a revitalizing of the applied arts and he pled for a new evaluation in which industry could be accepted on an equal footing with the beaux-arts as an equal expression of man's creative impulse:

> Les arts, les lettres, les sciences, le vêtement de son corps, l'ameublement de sa demeure, sont autant de branches de son industrie, considérées dans la juste extension du mot. L'art embrasse, donc, toute l'activité de l'homme.[2]

(Art, literature, sciences, clothing of one's body, furnishing of one's home are many branches of creativeness considered in the true extension of the word. Art embraces, then, the entire activity of man.)

The idea of wedding art and industry had been a moving force behind French industrial exhibitions since the late 1700s. But the growth of the middle class and its consumer demands made the matter more urgent. To counter the mediocre taste of the marketplace, Laborde outlined a three-fold program by which the state could educate the new consumers aesthetically. He recommended

1. See Phillip Dennis Cate and Sinclair Hamilton Hitchings, *The Color Revolution: Color Lithography in France, 1890-1900* (Salt Lake City: Peregrine Smith, 1978); Douglas Druick, "Books in Review: The Color Revolution: Color Lithography in France 1890-1900," *The Print Collector's Newsletter,* 10, no. 1. (March-April 1979): 25-26.

2. Léon de Laborde, *De l'union des arts et de l'industrie,* 2 vols. (Paris: Impr. imp., 1856) 2:2.

Figure 84. *French Company of Chocolates and Teas,* 1895, color lithographic poster (cat. 77).

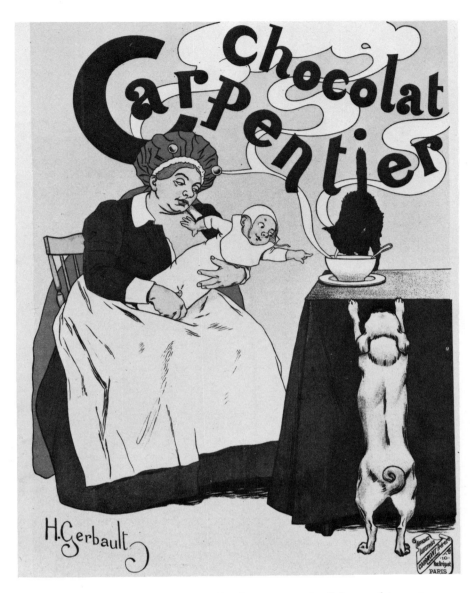

Figure 85. H. Gerbault, *Carpentier Chocolate,* 1895, color lithographic poster, illustration for *Les maîtres de l'affiche*. Courtesy Mr. and Mrs. Herbert D. Schimmel.

drawing for school children, specialized instruction in design for those who wished to pursue art professionally, and the improvement of public taste in architecture, museums, and public parades and festivals.

Laborde made little headway against a rigid and fully entrenched academic system with spokesmen like the artist Jean Auguste Dominique Ingres and conservative critics like Gustave Planche, until the 1889 Exposition Universelle in Paris. Then a fully fledged movement for the revival of the decorative arts emerged in France, and a decade later, at the Paris Exposition in 1900, the new movement, Art Nouveau, proved itself as a dominant force in French aesthetics.[3]

3. H.A. Needham, *Le développement de l'esthétique sociologique en France et en Angleterre au XIXe siècle* (Paris: H. Champion, 1926), pp. 167-69.

Figure 86. Jules Cheret, *Quinquina Dubonnet*, 1895, color lithographic poster.
Courtesy Jane Voorhees Zimmerli Art Museum.

While Laborde was championed by French critics as the apostle of the "new art," the British Arts and Crafts movement had a more immediate influence on the French. Throughout the 1890s and during the early twentieth century, books and articles appeared in France praising William Morris and the English decorative arts revival. Many French writers, including Gabriel Mourey, Jean Lahor, and Roger Marx, emphasized the democratic basis of the movement, another indication of the growing concern for the masses that characterized the period.[4]

The critic most responsible for bridging the gap between the decorative arts revival and the print and poster craze was the beaux-arts official Roger Marx. From 1889 until his death, Marx wrote numerous articles about art and society.[5] Like Morris and Laborde before him, Marx was outraged by the poorly made products of modern industry and by the dead imitation of past styles. The quality of life would be enhanced, he argued, by simple but well-made objects that reflected their own time, rather than senselessly quoting the past. Beautifully crafted everyday objects would enrich the life of the worker and the peasant and enhance human possibilities as never before.

Marx advocated the unity of the decorative arts and the fine arts, fought for greater status for the applied arts, and in 1891, saw the applied arts exhibited for the first time at the second annual Salon of the Société Nationale. In 1895, even the conservative *Salon des artistes français* included the applied arts at their yearly exhibition.

Figure 87. *Red Handed,* 1893, lithographic sheet music cover (cat. 67).

Marx's essay on prints included the preface to Ernest de Crauzat's catalogue of Steinlen's graphic art and five prefaces between 1895 and 1900 for the series *Les maîtres de l'affiche* ("The Masters of the Poster"), which issued major posters reproduced in a reduced format.[6] He saw posters as modern-day frescoes that enlivened the gray, uniform boulevards of Baron Haussman's Paris. Accessible to the common man outdoors, they also made inexpensive interior decorations. They were, in his view, the exemplary document of modern civilization.

4. See Jean Lahor, "M. William Morris et L'art décoratif en Angleterre," *Revue encyclopédique,* 4, no. 89 (15 Aug. 1894): 349-59; Gabriel Mourey, "William Morris," *Revue encyclopédique,* 6, no. 168 (1896): pp. 805-10. Both critics also wrote books on the subject: Lahor, *W. Morris et le mouvement nouveau de l'art décoratif* (Geneva: Eggimann, 1897); Mourey, *Passé le détroit: La vie et l'art à Londres* (Paris: P. Ollendorff, 1895).

5. Roger Marx, *L'art social* (Paris: Bibliothèque-Charpentier, 1913), pp. 50-51, a compilation of essays written between 1889 and 1913. See also his *La décoration et l'art industriel à l'exposition universelle de 1889* (Paris: Ancienne Maison Quantin, 1890).

6. See Marx, "Introduction" to Ernest de Crauzat, *L'oeuvre gravée et lithographiée de Steinlen* (Paris: Société de propagation des livres d'art, 1913), pp. ix-xv; and his prefaces in *Masters of the Poster 1896-1900* (New York: Images Graphiques, 1977).

Figure 88. *Mothu and Doria,* 1893, black and white lithographic proof for poster (cat. 73).

The poster was also the characteristic aesthetic product of Art Nouveau. The sinuous lines, flat areas of strong color, and pictorial abstractions common to this movement animated the works of Toulouse-Lautrec, Grasset, Mucha, and de Feure, to name a few of its exponents. Steinlen's prints and paintings contained no traces of Art Nouveau style, but his amazing technical virtuosity sent him experimenting with Art Nouveau aesthetics and thus placed his posters stylistically in the vanguard of *fin-de-siècle* French art.

Steinlen's earliest posters, those dating between about 1885 and 1891, were typical of the posters created from the 1860s through the 1880s. Diminutive figures and excessive details produced picturesque narratives. In 1893, however, he produced his first important poster, *Mothu et Doria*, a successful experiment in clarity of composition and simplicity of form (fig. 88).

Mothu and Doria were performers who often sang the repertoire of Albert Pajol, a lyricist and publisher who commissioned the poster and four sheet music covers from Steinlen. Mothu also appeared on the cover of a piece of music, *Sur le tas* ("Red Handed"), 1893 (fig. 87). He played the role of a vagabond, and Steinlen showed him in that role on both the sheet music cover and in *Mothu et Doria*. In the poster, however, Steinlen showed his shabby drifter getting a light for his cigarette from an elegant *aristo*. This forceful confrontation of social classes was a theme Steinlen had explored earlier in illustrations for *Le mirliton*. As we have seen, in 1894, it dominated his work for *Le chambard*.

Stylistically, *Mothu et Doria* represented a breakthrough. *Le rêve* ("The Dream"), a large-scale poster Steinlen did in 1891, came before that breakthrough. It was heavily infused with *japonaiserie*, a ballerina in the foreground acting

as a *repoussoir* ("foil").[7] Behind her clustered a large group of dancers whose tiny faces were barely perceptible. The details were complex, the perspective conventional and three-dimensional, and the depth came from both foreground and background shadows, all of which weakened and confused the poster's impact.

Mothu et Doria concentrated on only two figures who cover nearly the entire frontal plane of the composition. They appeared to stand out stark against an abstracted foggy night sky punctuated by street lamps. Steinlen used primarily red, yellow, black, and white. The vagrant's face was tinted reddish, while the streetlights poured out pure yellow. Steinlen had used *crachis* ("ink splatters") extensively to add texture, an advanced lithographic technique. The entire composition, including the flat outlined lettering, was forceful and attractive.

Mothu et Doria also showed the influence of Toulouse-Lautrec, whose first poster, *Moulin-Rouge*, appeared in 1891. In 1892 he published five posters, and in 1893 four more. His dynamic lines, emphatic outlines, and flattened forms were excitingly innovative. Steinlen had been interested in his colleague's work since 1888, when he included Toulouse-Lautrec's *Saint-Lazare*, a *Le mirliton* cover, in Bruant's book, *Dans la rue*. He also worked Lautrec's poster *Aristide Bruant dans son cabaret*, into his own June 1893 illustration for *Le mirliton* (fig. 89). Steinlen's *Mothu et Doria* borrowed the technique of silhouetting against a neutral

7. Steinlen had been aware of Japanese art at least since 1884 when he created for *Le chat noir* (19 July 1884) a page of cats in diverse poses that echoes a sheet of drawings from Hiroshige's *Ukiyo Ryusai Gwafu*. His 1888-89 drawings for *La semaine artistique et musicale* also reflect Japanese influence.

background with dynamic movement in the broad cape and red scarf from Toulouse-Lautrec.

Steinlen probably completed *Mothu et Doria* in the latter part of 1893—that is, after Toulouse-Lautrec's third poster of Bruant. A letter of Steinlen's to the printer dated 27 February 1894 asked for the return of his two lithographic stones and two hundred copies of the poster against 200 francs owed the artist for his services.[8] It would have been unlikely for Steinlen to have waited until the end of February 1894 for payment, if he had created the poster during the first half of the previous year.

Early in 1894, Steinlen produced his most celebrated poster, *Lait pur stérilisé de la Vingeanne* ("Pure Sterilized Milk from Vingeanne") (plate 20), for the company of Quillot Frères.[9] This was the first of several important commissions that Steinlen executed at the printing shop of Charles Verneau, later his principal printer. In *Lait pur* Steinlen created an innovation by showing a young blonde girl, his daughter Colette, sipping milk from a cup while three large cats, his pets, sat at her feet, gazing up absorbed at the milk. The poster established Steinlen as a masterful illustrator of cats. Until then—and primarily during the 1880s— Steinlen had drawn only small black cats for *Le chat noir*. Other artists during this period sometimes put cats on posters but not as effectively (fig. 85). Chéret's 1888 poster for Adolphe Willette's exhibition included a black cat stalking an artist's paintbox—an allusion to the café Chat Noir, with which Willette was associated. Chéret also included a white cat in *Quinquina Dubonnet*, 1895, to balance the puffy white feather in the hat of Chéret's model (fig. 86). A George Meunier poster of 1894 used a cat as a decorative device. Lucien Lefèvre,

Figure 89. Henri de Toulouse-Lautrec, *Aristide Bruant in His Cabaret,* 1893, color lithographic poster. Courtesy Mr. and Mrs. Herbert D. Schimmel.

8. Steinlen to M. Baume, 27 Feb. 1894, in possession of Marguerite Steinlen, Cergy, France.

9. A reduced version of this poster was issued by the British company, Waterloo and Sons, Ltd., for Nestle's milk. See Phillips Gallery Auction Catalogue, *Poster Classics,* (New York: Phillips Son & Neale, May 1980), no. 542.

Plate 15. *Mother and Child with Cat,* study for poster (fig. 90), oil on canvas (cat. 225).

influenced by Chéret in lettering background and bright colors, created an 1893 poster, *Cocoa Lacté* ("Cocoa with Milk"), that showed a small boy holding a bowl of cocoa away from a dog jumping for it.

The warm domesticity of Steinlen's poster and the logical association of cats and milk were successful concepts that added to the stylistic success of the design. The work fulfilled contemporary postermaking criteria: bright colors, prominent lettering, simple lines, and clarity of composition.[10] As in *Mothu et Doria*, Steinlen used yellow and red but without superimposing the darker tones. Colette's red dress and blond hair were broad, flat areas of color. Steinlen outlined with green lines (*verdâtre*) instead of black. This use created a soft effect against which the other colors stood out boldly. The poster's lettering appeared prominently at the top, drawn in a fluid "modern" script like the lines used to define the rest of the composition. The repetitive curvilinearity that defined the cats and emphasized the simplified lines of the main figure situated this work squarely in the context of Art Nouveau, which, in general, exhibited a tendency toward asymmetrical composition, a decorative quality evident in a concern for surfaces, and simplified, two-dimensional forms. Concern for the curvilinear dominated the posters of Grasset and Mucha.

Although Steinlen's style was not as ornamental as the work of these artists, Art Nouveau influence was also visible in several posters he made during this period. One of the most successful was *Compagnie française des chocolats et des thés* ("French Company of Chocolates and Teas"), a work of 1895 (fig. 84). Again, the artist included Colette and a cat. The woman at the left was probably based on Emilie, the artist's wife; she appeared in several other of his works. In *Lait pur*, the primary Art Nouveau element was the flowing curvilinearity of the three cats, but in *Compagnie française* the whole composition seemed

animated by energetic connecting lines. The uppermost compositional line moved uninterruptedly from mother to daughter to chair, and all elements in the work, particularly the woman and child, were defined by lively curves. This curvilinearity was echoed in the tabletop, a surface composed of negative space and shown in a radically cropped perspective. The energetic line, the tight interlocking forms, and the interest in negative and positive spaces were all characteristic of the Art Nouveau style.

In the following year, 1896, Steinlen produced a monumental poster measuring approximately 92 by 100 inches. *La rue* ("The Street") advertised Charles Verneau's printing shop (fig. 90). Fifteen nearly life-size figures formed a frieze on a Parisian street. In the center was Colette, led by a dark-haired woman who resembled the mother in *Compagnie française*. Along the frontal plane of the poster were a laundress, a young woman with a baby,[11] a well-dressed middle-class lady, a corpulent businessman, a milliner, and a *trottin* ("errand girl"). In the background were two laborers, an old woman, a nurse, and a man in a checked suit. The left side of this poster contained the sweeps, curves, and the movement typical of Art Nouveau. The figures on the right appeared almost wooden by comparison. The most prominent figure at the left is the laundress with a large laundry basket, her entire form defined with graceful curves that added tremendous vitality to the poster. She was surrounded by figures also composed of decorative sweeping lines. This was the most exciting part of the composition.[12]

10. Ernest de Crauzat, "Les estampes et les affiches du mois," *L'estampe et l'affiche* (Paris: E. Pelletan, 1898), p. 69.

11. Steinlen created an enamel of the woman and infant that he hung in the kitchen of his country home in Cergy where his niece, Marguerite Steinlen, now lives.

12. A sequel to *La rue, Le boulevard* was planned but never executed. "Artistic French Lithographs," *The Poster*, 1, no. 5 (Nov. 1898): 194. *La rue* was exhibited in April 1897 at the Salon de Figaro, an annex of *Le Figaro*, where posters were frequently shown. Crauzat, *L'estampe et l'affiche*, pp. 93, 127-38.

Figure 90. *The Street,* 1896, color lithographic poster (cat. 78).

Steinlen's posters treated women quite differently from those of his contemporaries.[13] Usually women added a sensual element in late nineteenth-century posters to attract the viewer. Chéret's fantastic and sexual women were integral to his concept of advertising. Grasset's women had the pre-Raphaelite allure of innocence. To some extent this was also true of Mucha, although his women were more overtly erotic. But Georges de Feure portrayed women as purveyors of evil, the epitome of *femmes fatales,* and Lautrec's performers were frequently embodiments of *fin-de-siècle* decadence.

In contrast, Steinlen ennobled the working woman. His portraits of the laundress and the *trottin* were rare instances of the working class appearing in posters of *la belle époque.* Except for the corpulent businessman who eyed the *trottin,* all of the figures in the foreground of *La rue* were women, and the three women on the left dominated the composition. The laundress, carrying her

13. See Jan Thompson, "The Role of Woman in the Iconography of Art Nouveau," *The Art Journal,* 31, no. 2 (Winter 1971-1972): 158-67; Robert Pincus-Witten, "The Iconography of Symbolist Painting," *Artforum,* 8, no. 5 (Jan. 1970): 56-62; Gabriel P. Weisberg, *Images of Women: Printmakers in France from 1830 to 1930* (Salt Lake City: Utah Museum of Fine Arts, 1977).

Figure 91. *Housewife and Children
Returning from the Laundry House,*
1899, etching, (cat. 8).

burden with ease and pride, was romanticized compared with later images of laundresses in Steinlen's art (fig. 91).[14]

The remaining women in the poster were also positive, linked to the female role of mother and nurturer. Even the milliner at the right walked close to her apprentice with maternal concern. The idea that maternity marked the virtuous woman was centuries old, but artists of the 1890s, among them Paul Gauguin, Maurice Denis, and Eugène Carrière created archetypal images of the "Good Mother."[15] Across the range of Steinlen's work, he dignified ordinary working women and mothers in a distinctive way.

14. See Eunice Lipton, "The Laundress in Late Nineteenth-Century French Culture: Imagery, Ideology and Edgar Degas," *Art History* 3, no. 3 (Sept. 1980): 295-313.

15. See Wendy Slatkin, "Maternity and Sexuality in the 1890s," *Woman's Art Journal* 1, no. 1 (Spring/Summer 1980): 13-19.

In the same year that he made *La rue,* Steinlen produced an iconic image of a cat for Salis's Chat Noir that was placed outside the renowned café (fig. 92). In this poster, Steinlen was probably influenced by *Gismonda,* the celebrated 1894 poster of Sarah Bernhardt, created by Czechoslovakian artist Alphonse Mucha (fig. 93). In Mucha's poster, Bernhardt stood on a corbel, like a great portal sculpture on a medieval cathedral. In a halo of light, her name appeared and, above that, the name of the play, *Gismonda.*

Steinlen's *Tournée du chat noir* ("Tour of the Chat Noir") was a good deal less ornate, but his black cat sat on a rough pedestal over which its tail was curled, much as Bernhardt's dress overlapped the sculptured corbel. The cat's head was surrounded by a halo bearing the inscription, "Mont Joye Montmartre." This medievalist style had originated in France with Eugène Grasset and became a fundamental aspect of Art Nouveau.

Figure 92. *Tour of Rodolphe Salis's Chat Noir,* 1896, color lithographic poster (cat. 79).

Figure 93. Alphonse Mucha, *Gismonda*, 1894, color lithographic poster, illustration for *Les maîtres de l'affiche*. Courtesy Mr. and Mrs. Herbert D. Schimmel.

Between 1896 and 1900 Steinlen produced ten more posters. Several of these continued the style of *Lait pur* and *Compagnie française*, displaying a flowing curvilinearity and closely knit figures. Most notable in this regard were *La traite des blanches* ("White Slavery") (plate 14), *Cocorico* ("Cockadoodledoo"), and *Motocycles Comiot* ("Comiot Motorcycles") (plate 16), all produced in 1899.

Several other posters from these years in different styles were notable. The first of Steinlen's political posters, *La feuille*, was printed in yellow, black, and white in 1897 for *La feuille* magazine (fig. 94). When the poster was issued, it was aptly described in *L'estampe et l'affiche*:

> *Comme les prospectus-réclames jetés, les jours de Mardi-gras et de Mi-carême, du haut des chars sur la masse compacte, béante des curieux et des badauds, le long des boulevards, La feuille voltigeant, s'éparpille sur un océan grouillant de têtes, officiers, bourgeois et prolétaires, proprios et ouvriers, à la grands joie des uns, au grand mécontentement des autres. On trouve dans cette affiche toutes les qualités maîtresses de Steinlen, science de la composition et du mouvement, vérité des types vécus et parfaitement rendus.*[16]

(Like the advertising handbills thrown on Mardi Gras and mid-Lent from the height of the floats onto the compact crowds, jammed with the curious and the strollers all along the boulevards, *La feuille* floats, scattered over an ocean of milling heads, officers, borgeoisie and proletariat, proprietors and workers, to the great joy of some and the great discomfiture of others. You will find in this handbill all the master qualities of Steinlen, a knowledge of the composition and movement, a truthfulness of characters lived and perfectly rendered.)

16. *L'estampe et l'affiche*, Nov. 1897, p. 227. The poster was published the previous month.

122

Figure 94. *La Feuille,* 1897, color lithographic poster (C.499).

La feuille was influenced by the work of several of Steinlen's contemporaries. In 1892, Maurice Denis had created a poster for *La Dépêche de Toulouse* ("The Toulouse Dispatch") in which sheets of the newspaper sailed down on an enthusiastic crowd, whose members reached up for them. Although Steinlen's crowd seemed rather assaulted by the anarchist notices, the compositions were similar. More important, though, was the influence of another artist and a compatriot of Steinlen's, Félix Vallotton, who had come from Steinlen's hometown, Lausanne, to Paris in 1882, a year after Steinlen. His black-and-white woodcuts produced from about 1893 depicted large crowds. They had been reproduced in popular magazines with which Steinlen was familiar and, in 1896, many were published in the book *Les rassemblements: physiologies de la rue,* edited by Octave Uzanne. In these works, Vallotton "flattened the image by eliminating the horizon line . . . and . . . cut . . . off heads in order to bring the figures up against the frontal plane of the pictures."[17] In most of the works, the faces of the people were barely indicated with a

17. Ashley St. James, *Vallotton: Graphics* (London: Ash & Grant, Ltd., 1978), 11.

Plate 16. *Comiot Motorcycles,* 1899, color lithographic poster (cat. 83).

Figure 95. *Paris*, 1898,
color lithographic
poster (cat. 81).

few dots and dashes, abstractions in keeping
with the avant-garde theories set forth by
Vallotton and his Nabi colleagues.

Steinlen's *La feuille*, printed primarily in
black and white, was filled with figures
arbitrarily cut off by the picture frame. While
the faces of those in the foreground were fairly
detailed, most of the figures—men in bowlers
and top hats—had a ghostly quality, abstract
but alienated, a possible echo from Edvard
Munch, whose lithograph *Anxiety* (which also
contained figures in top hats) appeared in
Vollard's 1896 *L'album des peintres graveurs.*

La feuille's faces were intended to satirize
the bourgeoisie, most prominently represented
in the foreground by a fat couple with beak-
like noses. An officer in the foreground might
have been a premonition of the Dreyfus affair,
which was to soon absorb the magazine. On
the right was a young blonde working woman
who stood beside a paper boy and looked
wistfully up at the sheets of paper. With youth
by her side, she possibly represented a more
harmonious future for the working class.

In two other major posters of the late
1890s women appeared as allegorical
personifications of Truth and Liberty. The first

of these was a poster for Zola's novel *Paris*
which was serialized in *Le Journal* in 1898 (fig.
95). *Paris* was the third volume of Zola's great
trilogy, *Rome, London, Paris,* and depicted such
aspects of Parisian life as the political
machinations of those in power and the
squalor of the poor. The book focused on the
anarchist Guillaume Froment, an idealist who
became involved in political violence. He is
Zola's device for analyzing ideals and the
shortcomings of anarchism.

Paris was originally planned in August
1897 as an extremely large poster but, because
of problems with space for posting bills, its size
had to be reduced. In September, Steinlen
wrote to his wife complaining that, after
ordering the canvas for this mammoth design,
he had had to begin all over again.[18] The
finished work, published in 1898, was, in fact,
one of Steinlen's largest posters. *Paris* had the
same dimensions (approximately 55 by 71
inches) as *La feuille, L'assommoir* and *Motocycles
Comiot* (plates 10, 16).

18. Steinlen to Emilie Steinlen, 27 Aug. 1897; Steinlen to
    Emilie Steinlen, undated. Steinlen correspondence in
    possession of Marguerite Steinlen, Cergy, France.

Despite Steinlen's frustrations, he created a powerful political image with a mythic view of the capital, seething with corruption, violence, and lust. In the background were the rooftops of the city and Sacré-Coeur surrounded by scaffolding, looming large on the horizon. The church, funded by a campaign by the fanatical Assumptionists, was conceived as a kind of national penance for the defeats of 1870-71. In Zola's novel, Guillaume plotted to blow up the church on the day of its opening ceremony.

Below this somber cityscape speckled with golden rays of light, a mass of naked bodies were locked in struggle. Their fierce arms and fists, ready to strike, rose up from the crowd. On the left, a large figure carried a jug over his head from which coins fell, as eager hands grabbed wildly for them. In the right foreground a savage-looking man grinned at the young girl he was embracing.

Truth rose above this heap of humanity in the form of a female nude with flowing hair. In 1893, Steinlen had already so represented Truth in a program for *La société républicaine des conférences populaires*. In that work, surrounded by masses of people, Truth advanced on a recoiling bishop. While the design anticipated *Paris* in some respects, the muscular proportions of the figures, their highly sculptural quality, the way in which they intertwined, the violence and the dramatic play of light and dark all recalled Rodin's *Gates of Hell*, which also had as its subject the moral dilemmas of society. It is unlikely that Steinlen had seen the maquette for the *Gates*, which Rodin showed to only a few friends in his studio. However, Steinlen could well have seen two large volumes of Rodin's drawings that were published in 1897 with a preface by Octave Mirbeau. Most of these drawings related to the *Gates* and were of muscular nude figures such as Steinlen drew in *Paris*.

If *Paris* was one of Steinlen's most visionary works, *Le petit sou* ("Small Penny"), 1900, was one of his most openly propagandistic (fig. 96). This poster, for the leftist periodical of the same name, showed Liberty with three workers descending on a large crowd that worshipped a golden calf in front of the Sacré-Coeur.[19] The church was armed like a fort with soldiers and cannons, symbolizing the partnership of Church and state. Not since his illustrations for *Le chambard* had Steinlen created anything that so fully embodied the revolutionary power of the workers.

La feuille, Paris, and *Le petit sou* all had definite political implications. For them Steinlen left Art Nouveau and used the style of his commercial works: book covers, sheet music covers, and commercial posters.[20] Of course, these three posters were made to sell a product, but they also represented Steinlen's leftist political thought. He may have felt, therefore, that a purely decorative style was inappropriate to such a sober purpose.

Steinlen also used a heightened realistic style in individual prints and murals created for numerous dealers and publishers involved in the print revival of the 1890s. Many of his finest prints appeared concurrently with his

19. Liberty is quite obviously based on Rude's *La Marseillaise*, 1833-36. In 1903, Steinlen repeated this image in a slightly different form in *La libératrice*, a print for Grave's *Les temps nouveaux*.

20. Probably the earliest work to display strong Art Nouveau tendencies was the sheet music cover for the song *Séparation*. It is dated 1892 by Crauzat, although it must have been completed at the end of that year, as a copy in the Bibliothèque Nationale is stamped 1893 by the Dépôt Légal. Later, in 1894, the artist created a related work for another song, *Déclaration*, by Georges Herbert and Alfred Bert. The same female figure appears in this cover, and again the composition is heavily infused with Art Nouveau elements. These elements appear sporadically in Steinlen's work through the second half of the 1890s. Two of the most notable examples were the book cover of 1895 for Fernand Vanderem's novel *Asche and Fanfreluches,* an illustration for Paul Delmet's *Les chansons de femmes* of 1897.

Figure 96. *Small Penny,* color lithographic poster (cat. 85).

Figure 97. *Caulaincourt Street,* 1896, lithograph (cat. 38).

most popular posters, yet they did not use the decorative grace of his posters. Two of the most impressive prints, both made for Kleinmann in 1895 and 1896, represented the world of prostitution, which Steinlen first illustrated in his work for *Le mirliton*. In *Filles et souteneurs* and *Dispute de filles,* the harshly planned faces of the prostitutes stood out against dense night shadows. If Steinlen had focused in the posters on line and color, in these black-and-white prints he emphasized mass and tone. When he was asked in the same year to contribute a lithograph to Andre Marty's series *Etudes de femmes,* he created an uncompromising portrait of a working woman. The harshness of working-class life is conveyed by the lines and scratches that define the grim expression of his *type populairé.*

In 1896, Steinlen produced *La rue Caulaincourt* for Löys Delteil's publication, *L'estampe moderne* (fig. 97). On a cold and windy night, two working-class men walked down a dark and deserted street—the street on which Steinlen actually lived. It was cold; the two solitary figures walked stiffly, their hands in their pockets, their collars upturned. The wind was represented by energetic lines that receded dramatically into the distance and by the angle of the two fighting their way forward.[21]

After 1900, Steinlen continued to produce drawings, lithographs, and etchings in this naturalistic style, but ceased to create posters with the decorative panache of the 1890s. By the turn of the century, posters were less popular and Art Nouveau was declining.

By 1900 Steinlen was at the peak of his fame and a source of inspiration to artists in Europe and America. Picasso, undoubtedly the most important painter to be affected by Steinlen's art, first learned of him in the gatherings of artists at the Barcelona café Els Quatre Gats, where Ramon Casas and Santiago Rusiñol led the Spanish modern art movement. Picasso was particularly taken with Steinlen's depictions of embracing lovers, but

21. *L'estampe moderne,* no. 4 (25 Feb. 1896). *La rue Caulaincourt* also appeared in the German periodical *Simplicissimus* 2, no. 18 (1897-1898).

Plate 17. *Lovemaking,* ca. 1920, watercolor (cat. 119, volume 3).

his *La mère* ("The Mother") (fig. 98) had a hitherto unrecognized similarity to Steinlen's *Ménagère et enfants rentrant du lavoir* ("Housewife and Children Returning from the Laundry House"), 1899. Picasso simplified the forms to heighten the expressive quality of his painting while Steinlen's image remained essentially illustrational. Yet the placement of the woman and the child whose hand she held, the silhouetting of the figure against the sky, and the inclusion of the buildings at the left, were all compositional devices shared by the two works. Even more striking, however, was the relationship of Picasso's *The Absinthe Drinker*, a major painting of 1901, and one of Steinlen's illustrations for *Gil Blas illustré*. In Picasso's painting, a woman with an extremely bony face, pointed chin, and long, thin fingers appeared in profile at the right of the canvas, sitting at a table with a glass of absinthe before her (fig. 99). The harshness of her life was reflected in her coarse features and in the distorted expression on her face. In the background were shadowy forms dressed in black that add foreboding to the scene. The woman's face, the position of her hands, and the atmospheric background were very similar to Steinlen's highly expressive portrayal of the prostitutes in *Les marcheuses*, 1893. The details of the foreground figure and the suggestive background in Picasso's painting were the "two fundamental components of the *modernista* painting developed by Rusiñol and Casas" in Spain, and explored by Picasso during his early years in Paris.[22] These elements were, undoubtedly, derived in part from a study of Steinlen's art.

Figure 98. Pablo Picasso, *The Mother*, 1901, oil on board. Courtesy St. Louis Art Museum.

22. Marilyn McCully, *Els Quatre Gats: Art in Barcelona around 1900*, (Princeton: Princeton University Press, 1978), p. 14. See Anthony Blunt and Phoebe Pool, *Picasso, The Formative Years: A Study of His Sources* (Paris: New York Graphic Society, 1962).

Figure 99. Pablo Picasso, *The Absinthe Drinker*, 1901, oil on canvas.

Steinlen was also highly regarded in the United States. Here, his *oeuvre* influenced the poster artists of the 1890s and the realists affiliated with the Ashcan school and with the periodical *The Masses*. Edward Penfield was a leading American postermaker whose art resembled Steinlen's in its clean lines and its everyday subject matter, shown by a comparison of his *Poster Calendar* (fig. 100), 1897, and Steinlen's *Compagnie française des chocolats et des thés*, about 1895. Penfield's negative space in the foreground to represent the table, the figure behind it, and the placement and treatment of the cat vividly recalled Steinlen's illustration. Another American poster artist whose work was influenced by Steinlen was Claude Fayette Bragdon. In his autobiography, Bragdon, later an architect and theatrical designer, discussed his admiration for Steinlen.[23] Bragdon's poster for *The Chap-Book*, 1895, was patterned after Steinlen's cover for Bruant's *Dans la rue* of 1888. In both works, men wearing sandwich boards advertised the publications.

Among the American realists, John Sloan was especially influenced by Steinlen as he acknowledged in his autobiography, *Gist of Art*.[24]

Sloan first became aware of Steinlen's work at about the turn of the century. In his paintings of streetlife, he represented a wide variety of New Yorkers in very much the same way that Steinlen had portrayed Parisians. In 1911, Sloan helped to found the left-wing periodical *The Masses* (1911-1916) whose contributors, in addition to himself, included George Bellows, Art Young, Robert Minor, Boardman Robinson, Maurice Becker, Glenn O. Coleman, and K.R. Chamberlain. The styles developed by these artists reflected their study of Steinlen and Forain. Sloan's images of rich and poor confronting each other on a New York street and those depicting young female office workers returning from work arm in arm were very much in the spirit of Steinlen's illustrations. Chamberlain's work showed an even greater dependence on Steinlen. Some of his images appeared to have been lifted directly from Steinlen's illustrations for *Gil Blas illustré* and *L'assiette au beurre*.[25]

23. Claude Fayette Bragdon, *More Lives than One* (New York: A.A. Knopf, 1938) p. 39. A photograph in the Bragdon file in the Art and Architecture Division of the New York Public Library shows Bragdon standing in front of Steinlen's poster, *A la bodinière*, 1894.

24. John Sloan, *Gist of Art* (New York: American Artists Group, Inc., 1939), p. 1.

25. For example, the figures in one of Chamberlain's illustrations for *The Masses*, January 1914, is based directly on a worker in a Steinlen illustration from *Gil Blas illustré*, 14 May 1893, p. 5. See Richard Fitzgerald, *Art and Politics: Cartoonists of the Masses and Liberator*, (London: Greenwood Press, 1973), for reproductions.

Figure 100. Edward Penfield, *Poster Calendar*, 1897, color lithographic poster.

Figure 101. Edward Hopper, *The Barrier,* 1915-18 (posthumous print), etching.
Courtesy Whitney Museum of American Art, New York.

Steinlen's impact on the younger realists was apparent in the early work of Edward Hopper. Although the French influence on Hopper has been well documented, Steinlen has not been mentioned as one of those influences before now. As a young illustrator, Hopper spent a good part of 1906-07 in Paris and made subsequent trips there in 1909 and 1910. About five years later, in 1915, he began to create etchings based on memories of his Parisian sojourns including a series of working-class men and women relaxing on the barricades that skirt the city of Paris. In *La barrière* ("The Barrier"), 1915-18, three solitary figures on a hill overlooked the city (fig. 101). The mens' caps and the woman's topknot hairdo located the image in the late nineteenth century. In 1923, in *Aux fortifications* ("French Couple on Embankment"), Hopper depicted larger groups of figures socializing atop similarly barren hills. A cruder version of this theme by Hopper might have been executed as early as 1906 (fig. 102). Steinlen had first portrayed pimps and prostitutes lolling about the Parisian fortress walls in his work for *Le mirliton* in the mid-1880s (fig. 103,104). He had, in fact, created a whole series of journal covers based on this theme, a theme no other artist used. Hopper probably saw these illustrations during his first visit to Paris when he was earning his living as an illustrator and would have been particularly sensitive to magazine illustrations by French artists. Furthermore, Hopper even echoed Steinlen's satirical quality, but in later prints on this theme Hopper emphasized the solitariness that would later dominate his work.[26]

26. See Gail Levin, *Edward Hopper: The Complete Prints,* (New York: Norton, 1979). The account of Hopper is taken from Levin's book. See also her article, "Edward Hopper, Francophile," *Arts Magazine,* 53 (June 1979): 114-121.

Figure 102. Edward Hopper, *French Couple on Embankment,* 1906-14, watercolor, ink, and conté crayon. Courtesy Whitney Museum of American Art, New York.

Figure 103. *The Goldbrickers,* cover illustration for *Le mirliton,* 1 September 1886, stencil colored photorelief. Courtesy Mr. and Mrs. Herbert D. Schimmel.

Picasso and Hopper were attracted to Steinlen's art because it embodied the "real" working-class Paris; it was perceived as honest and spontaneous. After Käthe Kollwitz met the artist in 1904, she wrote: "Besides Rodin, I visited Steinlen, the creator of *L'assiette au beurre*, in his studio. He, too, is someone I shall never forget. He was a typical Parisian. The loose tobacco in his wide pants pockets, his continual rolling of cigarettes, his wife, his many children[sic]—all combined to produce that Parisian atmosphere."[27]

One wonders, at that point, if she were the best person to recognize a typical Parisian. But whatever Steinlen's personal lifestyle, his ability to infuse his work with "Parisian atmosphere" was unquestioned. His illustrations recorded the dress, the gestures, and the manners of the people of Montmartre, and critics lauded his keen observation of contemporary life during his own lifetime:

> Le caractère principal de l'oeuvre de Steinlen, c'est l'étude approfondie des physionomonies et la reproduction de la vérité dans la pose and dans les détails . . . . Steinlen se distingue . . . par la beauté sociologique de son art . . . dans les types populaires qu'il a choisis, il a découvert ces traits généraux, ces nuances psychiques qui identifient entre eux tous les hommes.[28]

(The principal characteristic of Steinlen's work is his profound study of physiognomy and the reproduction of truth in the pose and details . . . . Steinlen is distinguished by the *sociological* beauty of his art . . . in the popular types he has chosen; he has discovered general traits, psychic nuances that distinguish one man from another.)

Steinlen's view of life was essentially optimistic. He believed deeply in man's ability to alleviate human suffering through kindness and justice. From the early 1880s through World War I, Steinlen's art was at the service of the underdog; he exposed and decried social inequities, motivated more by a deep concern for humanity than by a commitment to any political system. His empathetic concern for humankind, unquestionably, was the quality that most strongly shaped Steinlen's art, and it was that quality in his art which a new generation of artists at the turn of the century so readily respected.

27. *The Diary and Letters of Käthe Kollwitz*, ed. Hans Kollwitz, trans. Richard and Clara Winston (Chicago: H. Regnery Co., 1955) p. 45.

28. Maurice Lenoir, "Steinlen et son oeuvre," *Le mirliton*, 15 Dec. 1895, p. 3; H. Fiérens-Gavaert, "Un Maître Affichiste: Steinlen," *Art et décoration*, July 1897, p. 19.

Figure 104. *Idyll,* cover illustration for *Le mirliton,* June 1887, stencil colored
photorelief. Courtesy Mr. and Mrs. Herbert D. Schimmel.

Exhibitions

The Jane Voorhees Zimmerli Art Museum
(Formerly University Art Gallery)
Rutgers University
New Brunswick, New Jersey
October 31-December 15, 1982

Milwaukee Art Museum
February 10-March 27, 1983

Frederick S. Wight Art Gallery
University of California, Los Angeles
April 19-May 15, 1983

Lenders to the Exhibition

Norma Bartman
The William Bartman Family
Mr. and Mrs. B. Gerald Cantor
Mrs. Susan Schimmel Goldstein
Michael and Marilyn Gould
Dr. and Mrs. Yale Kramer
Joseph F. McCrindle
Mr. and Mrs. Herbert D. Schimmel
The Art Institute of Chicago
The Art Museum, Princeton University
The Boston Public Library
Sterling and Francine Clark Art Institute,
    Williamstown, Massachusetts
The Fine Arts Museums of San Francisco
    Achenbach Foundation for Graphic Arts
Margot Flatau Art and Antique Gallery,
    Los Angeles
Grunwald Center for the Graphic Arts,
    University of California, Los Angeles
The National Gallery of Canada, Ottawa
The New York Public Library
Park South Gallery at Carnegie Hall
La Petit Palais, Geneva, Switzerland

This exhibition and catalogue have been supported by grants from the
Pro Helvetia Foundation in Switzerland, the National Endowment for the
Arts, a federal agency in Washington, D.C., and Norma Bartman, Los
Angeles.

The Zimmerli Art Museum is supported by an operating grant from
the Institute of Museum Services, a federal agency in Washington, D.C.

Plate 18. *Young Woman of the Street*, ca. 1895, oil on canvas (cat. 227).

Acknowledgements

This exhibition and catalogue began with the dedication and persistence of two Los Angeles women, Norma Bartman and Margot Flatau, who greatly admired Steinlen's art. They not only collected it but sought art institutions to sponsor this major United States exhibition. Norma Bartman's efforts elicited a grant from the Pro Helvetia Foundation in Zurich, Switzerland, which allowed her to evaluate the private and public holdings of Steinlen's work in the United States and to promote the idea of an exhibition with various museums. My previous work on Steinlen for the 1978 exhibition and publication *The Color Revolution: Color Lithography in France, 1890-1900,* and the emphasis of the Rutgers Collection on nineteenth-century French printmaking, made it seem quite appropriate that Rutgers should organize a Steinlen exhibition. Norma Bartman not only generously allowed me access to her collection and research materials, and reproduced much of that material for my use at Rutgers, but also, with the valuable assistance of L. Clarice Davis, produced the bibliography for this publication. Without her substantive support and encouragement this exhibition and catalogue would not have occurred. I am, indeed, most thankful for her intense involvement and dedication to this exciting project.

Here at Rutgers, I was ably assisted by Lynn Klima in the coordination of the catalogue and loans, while Stephanie Grunberg, curator of education, Marguerite Santos, office and business manager, Anne Schneider, typist, Marilyn Tatrai, registrar, Jeffrey Wechsler, curator of painting and sculpture, and Dianne Witherbee, preparator, were instrumental in the complete realization of this project.

I am most appreciative of those who lent art to the exhibition. Dr. Oscar Ghez, director of the Petit Palais in Geneva, very graciously permitted thirty-four paintings, drawings, and prints from his amazing collection of over three hundred Steinlens to travel to the United States. The overwhelming cooperation of the following lenders from private and public collections was also most gratifying: Norma Bartman; Joseph F. McCrindle; Michael and Marilyn Gould; Susan Schimmel Goldstein; Dr. and Mrs. Yale Kramer; Mr. and Mrs. Herbert D. Schimmel; Harold Jaochim, curator of prints and drawings, the Art Institute of Chicago; Barbara Ross, custodian of prints, the Art Museum, Princeton University; Sinclair Hitchings, keeper of prints, and Eugene Zepp, assistant keeper of prints, the Boston Public Library; Joan Vita Miller, curator, the Cantor Foundation; Rafael Fernandez, curator of prints and drawings, the Sterling and Francine Clark Art Institute; Robert Johnson, curator, and Maxine Rosston, assistant curator for graphic arts, the Fine Arts Museums of San Francisco, the Achenbach Foundation; Margot Flatau, Margot Flatau Art and Antique Gallery; Maurice Block, the Grunwald Center for the Graphic Arts, UCLA; Douglas Druick, curator of prints, the National Gallery of Canada, Ottawa; Robert Rainwater, prints division, the New York Public Library; and Laura Gold, Park South Gallery.

Special thanks must go to Luc Boisonnas, director, and Christopher Eggenberger, head of exhibition service, of the Pro Helvetia Foundation, as well as to Pierre-Yves Simonin, cultural counselor, and Anna Widrig, secretary to the cultural counselor of the Swiss Embassy in Washington, D.C.

I am also very grateful to Herschel B. Chipp for his enlightening introduction to the catalogue and to Susan Gill for her detailed analysis of Steinlen's aesthetics and of the social-political content of his journal illustrations. The research of these two scholars brings to us a much richer understanding of the complexity of the period and of the role Steinlen played.

The enthusiasm for this exhibition on the part of Gerald Nordland, director, and Verna Curtis, associate curator, of the Milwaukee Art Museum, and Edith Tonelli, director, and Jack Carter, acting director of the Wight Art Gallery at UCLA, have made it possible for the art of Steinlen to be appreciated in central and western parts of the United States.

This exhibition and publication have been supported in part by grants from the Pro Helvetia Foundation, Zurich, Switzerland; the National Endowment for the Arts, a federal agency in Washington, D.C.; and Norma Bartman, Los Angeles.

Phillip Dennis Cate

My two essays in this catalogue have been adapted from my dissertation, "Théophile Steinlen: A Study of His Graphic Art, 1881-1900," City University of New York, 1982. I would like to thank Donald Harvey, Robert Pincus-Witten, and especially Linda Nochlin, my dissertation advisor, for their valuable criticism and advice.

Susan Gill

Catalogue of Exhibition

Numbers 1-144 are organized according to
Crauzat's 1913 *catalogue raisoné* of Steinlen's
printed work. Numbers 145-239 include
printed work not listed in Crauzat, as well as
drawings, paintings and bronzes.
Measurements are in centimeters, height
preceding width.

Etchings and Drypoints.

1. *Laundresses Carrying Back Their Work* (*Blanchisseuses reportant l'ouvrage*), 1898 (C.22) (fig. 46). Color drypoint, aquatint and line etching 36x27. Norma Bartman.

2. *Girl and Pimp* (*Fille et souteneur*), 1898 (C.23) (plate 12). Color aquatint etching 24x12.2. Jane Voorhees Zimmerli Art Museum, David A. and Mildred H. Morse Acquisition Fund.

3. *The Shower* (*L'averse*), 1898 (C.24) (fig. 47). Aquatint etching and drypoint 24x12.2. The Art Institute of Chicago, The Charles Deering Collection 1927.5411.

4. *The Laundress* (*La blanchisseuse*), 1898 (C.25). Color aquatint etching and drypoint 24x12.2. The Art Institute of Chicago, The Charles Deering Collection 1927.5387.

5. *Model Reading* (*Modèle lisant*), 1898 (C.26) (plate 9). Color drypoint, aquatint and line etching 19x29.2. Michael and Marilyn Gould.

6. *Little Nocturn* (*Petit Nocturn*), 1898 (C.30^{ii}). Aquatint etching 16.9x9.8. Norma Bartman.

7. *Young Girl with White Collar* (*Fillette au col blanc*), 1898 (C.32). Aquatint and line etching 28.9x14.4. Norma Bartman.

8. *Housewife and Children Returning from the Laundry House* (*Ménagère et enfants rentrant du lavoir*), 1899 (C.33) (fig. 91). Softground and aquatint etching 35.6x26.5. Dedicated in red pencil on lower right margin "à Anatole France, Hommage d'affectueuse admiration, Steinlen." Norma Bartman.

9. *Quitting Time for Three Young Dressmakers* (*La Sortie des trois midinettes*), 1900 (C.34) (fig 51). Color drypoint 14.9x22.5. Jane Vorhees Zimmerli Art Museum, David A. and Mildred H. Morse Acquisition Fund.

10. *Quitting Time for Three Young Dressmakers* (*La Sortie des trois midinettes*), 1900 (C.34). Copper plate for cat. 9 14.9x20.2. Mr. and Mrs. Herbert D. Schimmel.

11. *Babbling Old Woman* (*La vielle jasante*), 1902 (C.43^{ii}). Drypoint 16.2x10. Norma Bartman.

12. *The Little Street Singers* (*Les petits chanteurs des rues*), 1902 (C.47). Drypoint and line etching 29.9x29.8. Norma Bartman.

13. *Vagabond in the Snow* (*Vagabond sous la neige*), 1902 (C.67^{iii}). Etching 23.8x15.1. Published outside the text in *Le livre et l'image,* April 1902. Jane Voorhees Zimmerli Art Museum.

13a. *Two Errand Girls* (*Les deux trottins*), 1902 (C. 65^{iii}). Drypoint and aquatint etching 22.7x14.9. Published outside of the text in *Le livre et l'image,* April 1902. Jane Voorhees Zimmerli Art Museum.

14. *The House on the Edge of Town* (*Maison à l'entrée du village*), 1902 (C.68) (fig. 49). Color drypoint, softground and aquatint etching 18.8x30.6. The Art Institute of Chicago, The Charles Deering Collection 1927.5420.

15. *Two Nude Models* (*Deux modèles nus*), 1902 (C.70). Softground etching 39x40. Grunwald Center for the Graphic Arts, University of California, Los Angeles.

16. *Lovers on a Bench* (*Amoureux sur un banc*), 1902 (C.71). Softground, aquatint and line etching 34.4x49.8. Norma Bartman.

17. *Road through a Town* (*Route traversant un village*), 1902 (C.81). Color softground etching 21.2x28.7. The Art Institute of Chicago, The Charles Deering Collection 1927.5425.

18. *Cat on the Floor* (*Chat sur le plancher*), 1902 (C.88[iv]) (fig. 50). Color drypoint, softground, and aquatint 15.2x25.4. The Fine Arts Museums of San Francisco, Achenbach Foundation for the Graphic Arts purchase, 1965 (1965.68.6).

19. *Woman in Profile Combing Her Hair* (*Femme de profil se coiffant*), 1902 (C.90) (fig. 48). Softground and aquatint etching 39.4x29.4. The Art Institute of Chicago, The Charles Deering Collection 1927.6278.

20. *Woman Asleep* (*Femme couchée*), 1902 (C.92). Softground and aquatint etching 29.4x29.5. The Fine Arts Museums of San Francisco, Achenbach Foundation for Graphic Arts purchase, 1965 (1965.68.44).

Lithographs

21. *Going Up Again the "Boul Mich"* (*En R'Montant le Boul Mich*), 1890 (C.128). Relief transferred from lithograph 38x28.7. Norma Bartman.

22. *The Bourgeois Scarecrow* (*L'Epouvantail bourgeois*), 1893 (C.131). Stencil colored photorelief 34.5x27.8. Cover for *Le chambard*, #2, 23 December 1893 (C.655). The New York Public Library, Print Collection, Astor, Lenox, and Tilden Foundations.

23. *The Scream of the Pavement!* (*Le cri des pavés!*), 1894 (C.137) (fig 77). Stencil colored lithograph 32.3x29.3. Reproduced typographically as the cover for *Le chambard*, #8, 3 February 1894 (C.665). Jane Voorhees Zimmerli Art Museum.

24. *March 18* (*Le 18 mars*), 1894 (C.143) (plate 11). Stencil colored lithograph 35.2x32.5. Reproduced typographically as cover for *Le chambard*, #14, 17 March 1894 (C. 665). The New York Public Library, Print Collection, Astor, Lenox, and Tilden Foundations.

25. *The Last Ambush* (*Le denier guet-apens*), 1894 (C.144) (fig. 14). Stencil colored lithograph 33.8x29.5. Reproduced typographically as the cover for *Le chambard*, #15, 24 March 1894 (C.665). The New York Public Library, Print Collection, Astor, Lenox, and Tilden Foundations.

26. *Today!* (*Aujourd'hui!*), 1894 (C.145) (fig. 74). Stencil colored lithograph 30.5x30.9. Reproduced typographically as the cover for *Le chambard*, #16, 31 March 1894 (C.665). The New York Public Library, Print Collection, Astor, Lenox, and Tilden Foundations.

27. *Tomorrow!* (*Demain!*), 1894 (C.146) (fig. 75). Stencil colored lithograph 31.5x30.7. Reproduced typographically as the cover for *Le chambard*, 1894 (C.665). The New York Public Library, Print Collection, Astor, Lenox, and Tilden Foundations.

28. *The Deputy in the Fields* (*Le député aux champs*), 1894 (C.147). Lithograph 30.2x29.8. Norma Bartman.

29. *The First of May* (*Premier mai*), 1894 (C.148) (fig. 58). Lithograph 40.2x62.4. Petit Palais, Geneva.

30. *The Opportunist Majority* (*La majorité opportuniste*), 1894 (C.151) (fig. 76). Lithograph 31x29.5. Norma Bartman.

31. *May, 1871* (*Mai, 1871*), 1894 (C.152) (fig. 60). Lithograph 34x28.5. Petit Palais, Geneva.

32. *Independence Day* (*Fête nationale*), 1894 (C.158). Lithograph 29.7x30.2. Norma Bartman.

33. *To the Real Poor: The Bad Rich* (*Aux vrais pauvres: Les mauvais riches*), 1895 (C.161). Lithograph 25x36.3. For the program of the party given on 10 February 1895 for "*La Soupe populaire de Saint-Fargeau*". Jane Voorhees Zimmerli Art Museum, David A. and Mildred E. Morse Art Acquisition Fund.

34. *Arguing Prostitutes* (*Dispute de filles*), 1895 (C.166) (fig. 13). Lithograph 40.2x32.2. Norma Bartman.

35. Cover for the French edition of Abel Hermant's *Asche*, 1895 (C.167). Color lithograph 20x26.5. Jane Voorhees Zimmerli Art Museum.

36. Cover for the French edition of Abel Hermant's *Nathalie Madoré*, 1895 (C.168) (fig. 40). Color lithograph 21x28. Norma Bartman.

37. Cover for the second edition of Aristide Bruant's *In the Street* (*Dans la rue*), 1895 (C.170) (fig.4). Color lithograph 21x27.3. Norma Bartman.

38. *Caulaincourt Street* (*La rue Caulaincourt*), 1896 (C.171) (fig. 97). Lithograph 25.2x35.8. Published in Löys Delteil's short-lived *L'estampe moderne* (not to be confused with the later more successful publication of the same name). The Boston Public Library, Print Department.

39. *Interior of a Street Car* (*Intérieur de tramway*), 1896 (C.173) (fig. 8). Lithograph 26.5x34.5. The Boston Public Library, Print Department.

40. *Popular Type* (*Type populaire*), 1896 (C.180). Lithograph 31.5x25.8. Petit Palais, Geneva.

41. *Rooster and Hens* (*Coq et poules*), 1896 (C.181). Lithograph 80.7x65. Published by *L'estampe murale*. Park South Gallery at Carnegie Hall.

42. *Cats* (*Chats*), 1896 (C.182) (fig. 42). Lithograph 80.2x64. Published by *L'estampe murale*. Park South Gallery at Carnegie Hall.

43. Cover for Paul Delmet's *Songs of Women* (*Chansons de femmes*), 1897 (C.183). Color lithograph 31.5x43. Park South Gallery at Carnegie Hall.

44. *The Franco-Russian Payment* (*Le terme franco-russe*), 1897 (C.200) (fig. 79). Lithograph 36.2x29.7. Norma Bartman.

45. *Ten Assassinations for a Penny* (*Dix assassinats pour un sou*), 1897 (C.201) (fig. 83). Lithograph 36.3x28.6. Park South Gallery at Carnegie Hall.

46. *One Robs in the Shelter of the Law* (*On Détrousse au coin des lois*), 1898 (C.211). Lithograph 37.8x28.7. Norma Bartman.

47. *Cats and Little Girl* (*Chats et fillette*), 1898 (C.215). Color lithograph 46x31.5. Cover for the album, *Des chats* (C.598). Norma Bartman.

48. *The Singer of the Woods* (*Le chanteur des bois*), 1899 (C.221). Lithograph 20.8x14.9. Published in Paul Delmet's *Chansons de Montmartre* (C.218-234). Norma Bartman.

49. *Little Henry* (*Menu Henriot*), 1901 (C.247). Lithograph 24.5x15. Norma Bartman.

50. *Paris at Night* (*Paris la nuit*), 1903 (C.251ⁱ). Lithograph 18.6x30.1. Cover without letters for Jehan Rictus's *Soliloques du pauvre* (*Soliloquies of the Poor Man*). Norma Bartman.

51. *The Liberator* (*La Libératrice*), 1903 (C.252) (fig. 54). Lithograph 39x49. The Fine Arts Museums of San Francisco, Achenbach Foundation for the Graphic Arts 1963.30.1493.

52. *Frontal Portrait from the Waist up of Maxime Gorki* (*Maxime Gorki à mi-corps de face*), 1905 (C.265) (fig 41). Color lithograph 63x48. The Art Institute of Chicago 1973.155.

53. *Summer: Cat on a Balustrade* (*L'été: chat sur une ballustrade*), 1909 (C.292) (fig. 43). Color lithograph 49.3x60.7. Jane Voorhees Zimmerli Art Museum, Gift of the Class of 1958, Fifteenth Anniversary.

54. *Winter: Cat on a Cushion* (*L'hiver: chat sur un coussin*) (C.293), 1909 (C.293) (plate 8). Color lithograph 49.3x59. Jane Voorhees Zimmerli Art Museum, Gift of the Class of 1958, Twentieth Reunion.

55. *The Buffoons* (*Les Polichinelles*), 1890 (C.359). Stencil colored lithographic sheet music cover 37.7x23.4. Norma Bartman.

56. *The Bohemian Saint* (*La Sainte bohème*), 1890 (C.363). Stencil colored lithographic sheet music cover 31x22.5. Norma Bartman.

57. *Everlasting Loves* (*Eternelles Amours*), 1890 (C.364). Stencil colored lithographic sheet music cover 30.2x20.5. Norma Bartman.

58. *Adrift* (*A la dérive*), 1890 (C.366). Stencil colored lithographic sheet music cover 30x21. Norma Bartman.

59. *Good Evening* (*Bonsoir*), 1890 (C.369). Stencil colored lithographic sheet music cover 29.9x20.8. Norma Bartman.

60. *The Cherry Trees* (*Les cerisiers*), 1890 (C.370). Stencil colored lithographic sheet music cover 30.6x21.8. Norma Bartman.

61. *Huckleberry, The Woman of Montmartre* (*Airelle, la Montmartroise*), 1890 (C.371). Stencil colored lithographic sheet music cover 29.5x20.7. Norma Bartman.

62. *And That is Why, Madeleine or The Truant (Et voilà pourquoi, Madeleine ou L'ecole bussonière)*, 1890 (C.383). Stencil colored lithographic sheet music cover 26x16.6. Norma Bartman.

63. *The Dream of an Errand Girl (Le rêve de trottin)*, 1892 (C.408ii). Stencil colored lithographic sheet music cover 26x16.3. Norma Bartman.

64. *The "Ankou" (L'"Ankou")*, 1892 (C.414). Lithographic sheet music cover 26.6x16.8. Norma Bartman.

65. *Flirt (Muguette)*, 1892 (C.415ii) (fig. 32). Color lithographic sheet music cover 27.5x19.5. Jane Voorhees Zimmerli Art Museum.

66. *The Cytherean Batallion (Le Bataillon de Cythère)*, 1892 (C.419). Stencil colored lithographic sheet music cover 26.2x16.7. Norma Bartman.

67. *Red Handed (Sur le tas)*, 1893 (C.426i) (fig. 87). Lithographic sheet music cover 25.7x19. Norma Bartman.

68. *The Mashers (Les suiveurs)*, 1893 (C.428). Stencil colored lithographic sheet music cover 26.1x18.5. Norma Bartman.

69. *The Raid (La rafle)*, 1894 (C.446). Stencil colored lithographic sheet music cover 26.6x18.0. Norma Bartman.

70. *Mamma (Maman)*, 1894 (C.447iii). Stencil colored lithographic sheet music cover 26.4x17.5. Norma Bartman.

71. *The Organ Player (La Joueuse d'orgue)*, 1894 (C.449ii). Stencil colored lithographic sheet music cover 27.2x18.2. Norma Bartman.

72. *Woman of Sorrow (Femme de chagrin)*, 1894 (C.454i). Stencil colored lithographic sheet music cover 27.2x18.2. Jane Voorhees Zimmerli Art Museum.

Posters

73. *Mothu and Doria (Mothu et Doria)*, 1893 (C.490) (fig. 88). Lithographic poster (black and white proof) 129x94. Norma Bartman.

73a. *Mothu and Doria (Mothu et Doria)*, 1893 (C.490). Reduced version of the poster for *Les maîtres de l'affiche* series 26x20. Norma Bartman.

74. *Pure Sterilized Milk from the Vingeanne Region (Lait pur stérilisé de la Vingeanne)*, 1894 (C.491). Color lithographic poster 139x100. The Bartman Family.

75. *Exhibition of Drawings and Paintings by T.A. Steinlen (Exposition de l'oeuvre dessinée et peinte de T.A. Steinlen,*, 1894 (C.492) (fig. 19). Color lithographic poster 61x83. Jane Voorhees Zimmerli Art Museum, Gift of Mr. and Mrs. Herbert D. Schimmel.

76. *Yvette Guilbert Ambassadeurs*, 1894 (C.493). Color lithographic poster 187x79. Barbara Bartman.

77. *French Company of Chocolates and Teas (Compagnie française des chocolats et des thés)*, 1895 (C.494) (fig. 84). Color lithographic poster 80x60. Park South Gallery at Carnegie Hall.

78. *The Street (La rue)*, 1896 (C.495) (fig. 90). Color lithographic poster 238x304. National Gallery of Canada, Ottawa.

79. *Tour of Rodolphe Salis's Chat Noir (Tournée du chat noir de Rodolphe Salis)*, 1896 (C.496) (fig.92). Color lithographic poster 140x99. Jane Voorhees Zimmerli Art Museum, Gift of Susan Schimmel Goldstein.

80. *Hellé*, 1896 (C.497). Color lithographic poster 75.8x58.3. Jane Voorhees Zimmerli Art Museum.

81. *Paris*, 1898 (C.501) (fig. 95). Color lithographic poster 140x200. Park South Gallery at Carnegie Hall.

82. *White Slavery (La traite des blanches)*, 1899 (C.503) (plate 14). Color lithographic poster 160x125. Norma Bartman.

83. *Comiot Motorcycles (Motocycles Comiot)*, 1899 (C.505) (plate 16). Color lithographic poster 200x140. Dr. and Mrs. Yale Kramer.

84. *The Mysteries of the Pointed Tower (Les mystères de la tour pointue)*, 1899 (C.506). Color lithographic poster 80x60. Park South Gallery at Carnegie Hall.

85. *Small Penny (Petit sou)*, 1900 (C.507) (fig. 97). Color lithographic poster 135x96. Petit Palais, Geneva.

86. *The Trap (L'assommoir)*, 1900 (C.508) (plate 10). Color lithographic poster 200x140. William S. Bartman.

87. *Chéron Veterinary Clinic (La clinique Chéron)*, 1905 (C.511) (fig. 36). Color lithographic poster 197x140. Park South Gallery at Carnegie Hall.

88. *Arab Racahout (Racahout des Arabes)*, 1905 (C.512). Color lithographic poster before letters 65x50. Norma Bartman.

Photomechanically Illustrated Books, Prints, and Posters

89. *The Beggars' Song (La chanson des gueux)*, 1910 (C.519). Thirty-five lithographs plus one drawing within a Marius Michel binding 34x25.5. This group of lithographs is the preliminary effort by Steinlen for Richepin's *La chanson des gueux* (see cat. 119). The book initially was to be illustrated with 216 lithographs. Steinlen, however, only completed these thirty-five, of which this is the only complete set. *La chanson des gueux* was finally published with 252 illustrations reproduced photomechanically after drawings by Steinlen. Crauzat lists only twenty-four lithographs from the set. Norma Bartman.

90. *Dance on the Outskirts of Town (Bal de barrière)*, 1898 (C.520) (fig. 20). Colored collotype 21.1x34.7. Published by *L'estampe moderne*. Margot Flatau.

91. *The Dream (Le rêve)*, 1891 (C.529) (fig. 35). Color photorelief 31x60. Jane Voorhees Zimmerli Art Museum, Gift of Mr. and Mrs. Allan Maitlin.

92. Cover for Georges Courteline's *The Women of Amis (Les femmes d'Amis)*, 1887 (C.545). Stencil colored photorelief 22x13. Norma Bartman.

93. Cover for Aristide Bruant's *In the Street (Dans la rue)*, 1888 (C.549) (fig. 31). Stencil colored photorelief 18.7x24.8.

93a,b. *In the Street (Dans la rue)*, 1888 (C.549). Book (2 paper bound copies) 18.7x11.7. Songs and monologues by Aristide Bruant with 113 photorelief illustrations after drawings by Steinlen. Published by A. Bruant, Paris. Norma Bartman.

94. *In the Street (Dans la rue)*, 1888 (C.549) (fig. 24). Book 18.7x11.7. Title page illustrated by Steinlen in watercolor and ink. Dedicated in ink "à Lautrec." Verse written in ink by Aristide Bruant and watercolor sketch by Steinlen. Mr. and Mrs. Herbert D. Schimmel.

95. Cover for Camille Lemonnier's *The Comedy of Toys (La comédie des jouets)*, 1887 (C.550). Stencil colored photorelief 31.3x23.5. Published by Piaget, Paris. Norma Bartman.

96. Cover for E. Begout and Charles Malato's *Prison—End of the Century (Prison fin de siècle)*, 1891 (C.558). Color photorelief 20x27. Published by Charpentier and Fasquelle, Paris. Norma Bartman.

97. Cover for Octave Pradels's *Gallic Desserts (Les desserts gaulois)*, 1891 (C.560). Stencil colored photorelief 22.5x31. Published by Flammarion, Paris. Norma Bartman

98. *Aristide Bruant*, 1893 (C.563). Photorelief book 18x14. Text by Oscar Méténier. Thirty-one photorelief illustrations after drawings by Steinlen. Published by Le mirliton, Paris. Mr. and Mrs. Herbert D. Schimmel.

99. *Love Songs (Chansons d'amour)*, 1893 (C.564). Photorelief 12x18. Text by Maurice Boukay. Preface by Paul Verlaine. Nine photorelief illustrations after drawings by Steinlen. Published by Dentu, Paris. Mr. and Mrs. Herbert D. Schimmel.

100. *Catalogue of the First Exhibition of the Drawings and Paintings of Th.-A. Steinlen (Catalogue de l'oeuvre dessinée et peinte de Th.-A. Steinlen)*, 1894 (C.566). Photorelief 18x13. The exhibition was held at La Bodinière, 10 April-15 May 1894. Mr. and Mrs. Herbert D. Schimmel.

101. *Invitation to the First Exhibition of the Work of Th.-A. Steinlen*, 1894. Color photorelief 14.5x7.8. Inscribed to Alfred Stevens. Norma Bartman.

102. Cover for Georges Courteline's *Ah! Youth! . . . (Ah! Jeunesse! . . .)*, 1894 (C.568). Stencil colored photorelief 19.5x28.5. Published by Flammarion, Paris. Norma Bartman.

103. Cover for Georges Brandimbourg's *Sketch of Vice (Croquis du vice)*, 1895 (C.575). Two-toned stencil colored photorelief 18.8x28. Published by Antony and Company, Paris. Norma Bartman.

104,104a. *In the Street* (*Dans la rue*), 1895 (C.576) (fig. 15,23,25). Book (2 copies) 18.2x11.7. Songs and monologues by Aristide Bruant with 148 photorelief illustrations after drawings by Steinlen. Norma Bartman.

105. Cover for Zo d'Axa's *From Mazas to Jerusalem* (*De Mazas à Jérusalem*), 1895 (C.577) (fig. 78). Stencil colored photorelief 42x27. Norma Bartman.

106. Cover for Georges Courteline's *A Serious Customer* (*Un client sérieux*), 1897 (C.589) (fig. 67). Stencil colored photorelief 19x13.5. Published by Flammarion, Paris. Norma Bartman.

107. *The Childish Encyclopedia,* (*L'encyclopédie enfantine*), ca. 1897 (C.590). Two booklets, color photorelief. Fourth series: *Crazy Day* (*Folle journée*) 18.3x13.8. Fifth series: *Blockhead* (*Gribouille*) 16.7x12. Norma Bartman.

108. *Songs of Women* (*Chansons de femmes*), 1897 (C.594) (fig. 16). Book 28x19. By Paul Delmet. Preface by Armand Sylvestre. Fifteen full page photorelief illustrations after lithographs by Steinlen (C.183-197), published by Enoch and Company, P. Ollendorf, Paris. Norma Bartman.

109. Cover for Maurice Boukay and Marcel Legay's *Red Songs* (*Chansons rouges*), 1897 (C.596) (fig. 34). Color lithograph 18.7x13.2. Published by Flammarion, Paris. Norma Bartman.

110. *Songs of Montmartre* (*Chansons de Montmartre*), 1898 (C.597). Book 25x33.5. By Paul Delmet. Preface by Maurice Boukay. Fifteen full page photorelief illustrations after lithographs by Steinlen (C.218-231) and eighteen vignettes printed from relief plates. Published by Flammarion, Paris. Mr. and Mrs. Herbert D. Schimmel.

111, 111a. *Some Cats* (*Des chats*), 1898 (C.598) (fig. 18). Book (two copies) 44x30.5. Twenty full page photorelief "stories without words" by Steinlen, originally published in *Le chat noir*. Published by Flammarion, Paris. Norma Bartman.

112. *Stories for Sarah* (*Contes à Sarah*), 1899 (C.604). Book 16x24. Ten "stories without words" by Steinlen. Originally published in *Le chat noir*. Wood engraved by A. Desmoulins. Published by Carteret, Paris. Mr. and Mrs. Herbert D. Schimmel.

113. *Story of Brisquet's Dog* (*Histoire du chien de Brisquet*), 1900 (C.613). Book 23x28.5. By Charles Nodier. With a letter to Jeanne from Anatole France. Twenty-five drawings by Steinlen. Wood engraved by Deloche, Froment, Ernst and Frederic Florian. Published by Edouard Pelletan, Paris. Norma Bartman.

114. *The Crainquebille Affair* (*L'affaire Crainquebille*), 1901 (C.615). Journal 30x20. Number 14 of the *L'illustration théâtrle*, 19 August 1905. Illustrated with sixty-three wood engravings after drawings by Steinlen. Norma Bartman.

115. *Book-lover's Almanac* (*Almanach du bibliophile*), 1901 (C.616). Book 20x14. Thirty-one wood engraved illustrations by Froment after drawings by Steinlen. Published by Edouard Pelletan, Paris. Margot Flatau Art and Antique Gallery.

116. *The Characters of Bruant* (*Les types de Bruant*), 1902 (C.618). Book 12x18. Popular piece in one act, by Aristide Bruant and B. Lebreton. Color photorelief cover by Steinlen. Seventeen photorelief illustrations after the drawings originally published in the two volumes of *Dans la rue*. Mr. and Mrs. Herbert D. Schimmel.

117. *The Soliloquies of the Poor Man* (*Les soliloques du pauvre*), 1903 (C.624). Book 14x19. By Jehan Rictus. Revised edition corrected and augmented with unedited poems. 111 photorelief illustrations after drawings by Steinlen. Published by Sevin and Rey, Paris. Mr. and Mrs. Herbert D. Schimmel.

118. *The Miners* (*Les gueules noires*), 1907 (C.639). Book, color lithograph cover 23.6x18. Fifteen lithographs by Steinlen outside the text. Forty photorelief illustrations after drawings by Steinlen. Text by Emile Morel. Preface by Paul Adam. Published by E. Sansot and Company, Paris. Norma Bartman.

119. *The Beggars' Song* (*La chanson des gueux*), 1910 (C.643) (plates 1,4,16). Three volumes, each 34x25.5. Two hundred fifty-two photorelief illustrations after drawings by Steinlen. These three volumes plus cat. 120 contain two sets of proofs of the illustrations on china and japan paper, as well as a total of thirty-nine original watercolors and ink drawings which date from about 1920. The bindings were made by Marius Michel, each with an inlaid

leather design carved and colored by Steinlen. These volumes and cat. 120 are the second of three sets specially commissioned by collectors soon after the 1910 publication. This set belonged to Louis Barthou. Text by Jean Richepin. Published by Edition d'Art, Edouard Pelletan. Norma Bartman.

120. *The Last Songs of My First Book* (*Les dernières chansons de mon premier livre*), 1910 (C.644) (plate 4). Book 34x25.5. Twenty-four photorelief illustrations after drawings by Steinlen. See Note, cat. 119. Text by Jean Richepin. Published by Edition d'Art, Edouard Pelletan. Norma Bartman.

Journals

121. *Le chat noir* #126, 7 June 1884 (C.649). *In the Moonlight* (*Au clair de la lune*). Cover, photorelief 44.5x31. Norma Bartman.

122. *Le chat noir* #139, 6 September 1884 (C.649). *The Story of a Painter* (*Le roman d'un peintre*) (fig. 11). Photorelief 44.5x31. Margot Flatau.

123. *Le chat noir* #250, 23 October 1886 (C.649). *This Rascal Buffoon* (*Ce coquin de Polichinelle*). Cover, photorelief 44.5x31. Margot Flatau.

124. *Le mirliton* #52, November 1888 (C.652). *Drunkards* (*Soulauds*) (fig. 2). Stencil colored photorelief 27.5x17.5. Alexander Library, Department of Special Collections, Rutgers University.

125. *Le mirliton* #81, April 1892 (C.652). *In Vincennes Wood* (*Au Bois de Vincennes*) (fig. 3). Stencil colored photorelief 27.5x17.5. Alexander Library, Department of Special Collections, Rutgers University.

126. *Le mirliton* #101, 17 March 1893 (C.652). *The Black Cat* (*Le chat noir*). Stencil colored photorelief 38x28. Norma Bartman.

127. *Le mirliton* #141, 22 December 1893 (C.652). *Lovers* (*Amoureux*). Stencil colored photorelief 38x28. Alexander Library, Department of Special Collections, Rutgers University.

128. *Le mirliton* #5, 2 February 1894 (C.652). *Those in Luck's Way* (*C'qu'y sont veinards*) (fig. 21). Proof for cover illustration, stencil colored photorelief 38x28. Mr. and Mrs. Herbert D. Schimmel.

129. *Gil Blas illustré* #5, 3 February 1894 (C.660). *For a Night of Love* (*Pour une nuit d'amour*). Color photorelief 37.3x27.6. Jane Voorhees Zimmerli Art Museum, Gift of Mr. and Mrs. Herbert D. Schimmel.

130. *Gil Blas illustré* #8, 24 February 1895 (C.660). *Sharp Fellows of the Time* (*Fins de siècle*). Color photorelief 37.3x27.6. Jane Voorhees Zimmerli Art Museum, Gift of Mr. and Mrs. Herbert D. Schimmel.

131. *Gil Blas illustré* #22, 2 June 1895 (C.660). *End of the Idyll* (*Fin d'idylle*). Color photorelief 37.3x27.6. Jane Voorhees Zimmerli Art Museum, Gift of Mr. and Mrs. Herbert D. Schimmel.

132. *Gil Blas illustré* #11, 18 March 1898 (C.660). *At the Studio* (*A l'atelier*). Color photorelief 37.3x27.6. Jane Voorhees Zimmerli Art Museum, Gift of Mr. and Mrs. Herbert D. Schimmel.

133. *Gil Blas illustré* #13, 1 April 1898 (C.660). *The Errand Girls* (*Les trottins*). Color photorelief 37.3x27.6. Jane Voorhees Zimmerli Art Museum, Gift of Mr. and Mrs. Herbert D. Schimmel.

134. *Gil Blas illustré* #37, 16 September 1898 (C.660). *Nocturn* (*Nocturne*). Color photorelief 37.3x27.6. Jane Voorhees Zimmerli Art Museum, Gift of Mr. and Mrs. Herbert D. Schimmel.

135. *Le rire* #62, 11 January 1896 (C.672) (fig. 28). *At the Moulin de la Galette* (*Au moulin de la Galette*) by Steinlen and *Skating American Beauty* by Toulouse-Lautrec. Cover, color photorelief 30.7x23. Norma Bartman.

136. *Le rire* #70, 7 March 1896 (C.672). *So You Like Them Small Like That—You Lecher* (*C'est p'têt comme ça que tu les aimes—Satyre*). Photorelief 30.7x23. Norma Bartman.

137. *Le rire* #72, 21 March 1896 (C.672). *Thursday of the 3rd Week of Lent* (*Passé la mi-carême*). Color photorelief 30.7x23. Norma Bartman.

138. *Paris*, 1898 (C.682). Color photorelief 52.8x39.8. Norma Bartman.

139. *Cocorico* #2, 15 January 1899 (C.684). Cover, color photorelief 23x29. Park South Gallery at Carnegie Hall.

140. *Cocorico*, 1899 (bound, one year) (C.684). Photorelief 23x29. Mr. and Mrs. Herbert D. Schimmel.

141. *L'assiette au beurre* #13, 27 June 1901 (C.691) (fig. 30). *The Issy Catastrophe (La catastrophe d'Issy)*. Cover, color photorelief 31.3x24.5. Norma Bartman.

142. *L'assiette au beurre* #129, 19 September 1903 (C.691). *Judicial Errors (The Loizemant Affair) (Erreurs judiciares (L'affaire Loizemant))*. Color photorelief 31.3x24.5. Norma Bartman.

143. *L'assiette au beurre* #137, 14 November 1903 (C.691). *The Two Justices (Judges and Judgers) (Les deux justices (juges et jugeurs))*. Color photorelief, 31.3x24.5. Norma Bartman.

144. *In Life (Dans la vie)* (C.708). Book and cover, color photorelief 14.5x19.6. Mr. and Mrs. Herbert D. Schimmel.

Works Not Included in Crauzat's Catalogue.

145. *The Portrait of Jules (Le portrait de Jules)*, 1881. Color photorelief 35.3x24. From *Imagerie artistique*, series 1, #13, 1881. The National Gallery of Canada, Ottawa.

146. *The Comical Tribunals (Les tribunaux comiques)*, 1888. Book cover, stencil colored photorelief 19.5x28.5. Text by Jules Moinaux. Published by C. Marpon and E. Flammarion, Paris. Norma Bartman.

147. *Pure Sterilized Milk of the Vingeanne Region (Lait pur stérilisé de la Vingeanne)* (C.491), 1894. Instructional cards 38x27. Park South Gallery at Carnegie Hall.

148. *Homage to Zola (Hommage à Zola)* (fig. 56), ca. 1902. Lithograph 37.5x34.8. The Art Institute of Chicago, The Charles Deering Collection 1927.5464.

149. *The Tenant (Le locataire)*, 1913 (fig. 37). Color lithographic poster 153x120. Norma Bartman.

150. *Belmont near Lausanne (Belmont près de Lausanne)*, 1914 (fig. 52). Drypoint 55x72. Petit Palais, Geneva.

151. *The Poor People (Les pauvres gens)*, 1914. Drypoint 39x33. Norma Bartman.

152. *Two Cats (Deux chats)*, ca. 1914. Etching 38x32.5. Park South Gallery at Carnegie Hall.

153. *The Mobilization (La mobilisation)*, 1915 (fig. 57). Etching 60x46. The Bartman Family.

154. *Three Soldiers Walking*, ca. 1915. Etching 15x9.4. The Bartman Family.

155. *Line of Five Soldiers*, ca. 1915 (fig. 53). Drypoint 37x58. The Bartman Family.

156. *The Republic Calls Us (La république nous appèlle)*, 1915 (fig. 59). Lithograph 55x68. Petit Palais, Geneva.

157. *The Day of the Doughboy (Journée du poilu)*, 25-26 December 1915. Photorelief postcard after a poster of the same image 13.8x8.8. Norma Bartman.

158. *Glory (La gloire)*, 1915. Color lithograph 29.7x41. The Boston Public Library, Print Department.

159. *Serbian Evacuees (Evacués serbes)*, 1916. Etching 28x48. The Bartman Family.

160. *Long Live Raemaekers! (Vive Raemaekers!)*, 1916. Lithograph 38x57. The Bartman Family.

161. *Transport of the Wounded (Transport de blessés)*, ca. 1916 (fig. 84). Lithograph 38x57. The Bartman Family.

162. *Two Friends (Les deux amis)*, ca. 1916. Lithograph 38x57. Park South Gallery at Carnegie Hall.

163. *Three Soldiers Waiting at the Station*, ca. 1916. Lithograph 29x42. The Bartman Family.

164. *The Two Processions (Les deux cortéges)*, 1916. Lithograph 45x60. The Bartman Family.

165. *Forced March*, ca. 1916 (fig. 44). Lithograph 52x67. The Bartman Family.

166. *Soldier Leaving Family*, 1916. Lithograph 56x38. The Bartman Family.

167. *National Aid (Le secours national)*, ca. 1916. Lithograph 37.5x52. The Bartman Family.

168. *Soldiers on Leave (Permissionnaires)*, ca. 1916. Lithograph 41x60. The Bartman Family.

169. *The Social Duty (Le devoir social)*, 1917 (fig. 39). Color lithographic poster 44x30. The Bartman Family.

170. *The Devastated Aisne (L'Aisne dévastée),* 1917. Lithographic poster 110x79. The Bartman Family.

171. *The Painter on the Hill (Le Peintre sur la butte),* 1922. Drypoint 13.9x11.3. Norma Bartman.

172. Untitled, 1922 (fig. 38). Color lithographic poster 77.5x58. Norma Bartman.

173. *Cat (Chat),* no date. Color stencil 10.2x29.2. Jane Voorhees Zimmerli Art Museum.

Drawings and Watercolors

174. *Saint Saucepan (Sainte-Marmite),* 1886. Ink and watercolor 14x24. Cover for *Le mirliton,* 15 January 1886. Mr. and Mrs. Herbert D. Schimmel.

175. *The Two Coachmen (Les deux cochers)* (fig. 64). Ink 47.5x30.5. Illustration for *Le chat noir,* #238, July 1886. Petit Palais, Geneva.

176. *In Love (Amoureux)* (fig. 65). Ink and blue crayon on Gillot paper with collage 17.5x18. Illustration for *Dans la rue,* 1888 (C.549). Joseph F. McCrindle.

177. *At Montrouge (A Montrouge)* (fig. 33). Pen and ink with white gouache and blue pencil collage 25.5x16.5. Illustration for *Dans la rue,* 1888 (C.549). Norma Bartman.

178. *Sweepers,* 1888. Ink and blue crayon on Gillot paper 30x24. Joseph F. McCrindle.

179. *Pilon,* 1888. Blue crayon, wash and brown ink 34x23. Joseph F. McCrindle.

180. *Bittersweet (La joie triste)* (fig. 17), 1892. Pen and crayon 30x24. Illustration for *Gil Blas,* #9, 28 February 1892. Mr. and Mrs. Herbert D. Schimmel.

181. *In Vincennes Wood (Au Bois de Vincennes),* 1892. Watercolor 28x22. Reproduced on the cover of *Le mirliton,* #81, April, 1892. Petit Palais, Geneva.

182. *The Little Sorrow (Le petit chagrin).* Pen and crayon 17.5x13.5. Reproduced on the cover of *Gil Blas,* #27, 3 July 1892. Petit Palais, Geneva.

183. *Loie Fuller,* 1892. Blue crayon 28x23. Study for cover of *Gil Blas,* #52, 25 December 1892. Mr. and Mrs. Herbert D. Schimmel.

184. *Independence Day (Fête nationale),* 1894. Pastel 43.5x40. Study for C.158, published in *Le chambard,* 14 July 1894. Park South Gallery at Carnegie Hall.

185. *Half-beavers (Demi-castors)* (fig. 26), 1894. Ink and crayon 43x34. Reproduced on the cover of *L'echo de Paris* (C.667), 1894. Served as an announcement of the novel by Oscar Méténier. Petit Palais, Geneva.

186. *Study for the 1st of May (Etude pour le 1er Mai),* 1894. Color pencil 45x39. The Art Museum, Princeton University, Platt Collection.

187. *The 1st of May (Le premier mai),* ca. 1894. Ink and crayon 29x40. Petit Palais, Geneva.

188. *Aristide Bruant,* 1895 (fig. 68). Crayon 33x26. Reproduced on cover of *Le mirliton,* 15 November 1895. Mr. and Mrs. Herbert D. Schimmel.

189. *The Madpeople (Les fous),* 1895 (plate 13). Watercolor and ink 29x23. Reproduced on the cover of *Gil Blas,* #50, 15 December 1895. Petit Palais, Geneva.

190. *Bread Carrier (La porteuse de pain),* 1895 (plate 3). Pastel 49x43. Petit Palais, Geneva.

191. *End of the Idyll (Fin d'idylle),* 1895 (fig. 69). Pastel 37x30. Reproduced on the cover of *Gil Blas,* 2 June 1895. Petit Palais, Geneva.

192. *Men Watching,* ca. 1895. Blue crayon 17x20. Study for illustration in *Dans la rue* (C.576), pp. 176-77. Norma Bartman.

193. *Yvette Guilbert,* 1896. Drawing with wash 35x27. Study for illustration in *Le rire,* #70, 7 March 1896. Sterling and Francine Clark Art Institute, Williamstown, Massachusetts.

194. *Two Honest Women (Deux honnêtes femmes)* (fig. 27), 1896. Ink and crayon 33.5x26.5. Reproduced on cover of *Gil Blas,* #19, 8 May 1896. Petit Palais, Geneva.

195. *There Have to be Women (Faut des femmes),* 1896. Ink and pastel 52x25. Reproduced on back page of *Gil Blas,* #27, 3 July 1896. Petit Palais, Geneva.

196. *The Lovers (Les amoureux),* 1901. Pastel 56x74. Reproduced in *L'assiette au beurre,* #7, 16 May 1901. Mr. and Mrs. B. Gerald Cantor.

197. *Woman in Doorway*, 1902. Crayon 50x15. Study for *Sur le seuil* (C.44). Norma Bartman.

198. *March 18th at Père Lachaise Cemetery* (*Le 18 mars au Père Lachaise*) (fig. 29), 1903. Chalk and wash 30x42. Reproduced in *Le canard sauvage*, #1, 21 March 1903. B. Gerald Cantor.

199. *The Return from Longchamp* (*Le retour de Longchamp*), ca. 1903. Charcoal and blue pencil 32x23. Norma Bartman.

200. *The Natural Pimp of Judges* (*Le souteneur naturel des jugeurs*) (fig. 66), 1903. Crayon 39x32. Reproduced on back cover *L'assiette au beurre*, #137, 14 November 1903. Joseph F. McCrindle.

201. *Street Scene* (*Scène de rue*), 1904. Watercolor 161x221. Petit Palais, Geneva.

202. Study for *Chéron Veterinary Clinic* (*La clinique Chéron*) (C.511), 1905. Watercolor, pastel, and pencil 190x137. Anonymous.

202a. Study of dogs for *Chéron Veterinary Clinic* (*La clinique Chéron*) (C.511), 1905. Two-sided pencil drawing 46x60. Jane Voorhees Zimmerli Art Museum, Gift of Sanford and Myra Kirschenbaum.

203. *Liberty Leading Soldiers*, 1914. Study for a lithograph, charcoal 47x30. Joseph F. McCrindle.

204. *Three Soldiers*, ca. 1915. Crayon 37x25.5. The Bartman Family.

205. *Café Scene*, no date. Charcoal and blue pencil 50x40. Norma Bartman.

206. *Large Grocery Store, Street of the Abbess* (*Grande épicerie, rue des Abbesses*), no date. Blue crayon 38x28. Norma Bartman.

207. *Horse and Cab*, no date. Pastel 14.5x18.5. Margot Flatau.

208. *The Procession* (*Le cortège*), no date. Charcoal and pastel 35.7x27.5. The Art Institute of Chicago, Gift of Frank B. Hubachek 1965.28.

209. *Let's Stab Marianne* (*Poignardons Marianne*) (fig. 55), no date. Pastel 42x34.5. Petit Palais, Geneva.

210. *Two Women & Man's Head*, no date. Charcoal 19x22. Norma Bartman.

211. *Sketchbook Page* (fig. 45), no date. Ink, double-sided 30x52.5. Norma Bartman.

212. *Two Actors; Mevisto and Gemier*, no date. Crayon 30.5x28. Norma Bartman.

213. *Three Cats*, no date. Pencil 21x23. Norma Bartman.

214. Double-sided drawing. Recto: *Man in Top Hat*; Verso: *Female Figure, Dressed*; no date. Recto—watercolor, Verso—charcoal 35x27. Norma Bartman.

215. *Seated Woman in Dressing Gown* (*Femme assise au peignoir*) (fig. 62), no date. Charcoal and chalk on blue paper 47x60. Michael and Marilyn Gould.

216. *Reclining Nude* (*Nu couché*) (fig. 63), no date. Charcoal and chalk 47x60. Michael and Marilyn Gould.

217. *Rodolphe Salis at the Chat Noir Cabaret* (*Rodolphe Salis au cabaret du Chat noir*) (plate 2), ca. 1884. Watercolor 45.5x34. Petit Palais, Geneva.

Paintings

218. *Louise-Michel on the Barricades* (*Louise-Michel sur les barricades*) (plate 5), ca. 1884. Oil on canvas 112x86. Petit Palais, Geneva.

219. *Street Scene* (*Scène de rue*), 1888. Oil on panel 21x27. Petit Palais, Geneva.

220. *The Black Cat Gaudeamus* (*Le chat noir Gaudeamus*) (fig. 61), ca. 1890. Oil on canvas 172x84. Petit Palais, Geneva.

221. *In the Horse-drawn Coach* (*Dans la diligence à chevaux*) (plate 7), 1890. Oil on canvas 60x81. Petit Palais, Geneva.

222. *The Bread Carrier* (*La porteuse de pain*) (fig. 5), 1892. Oil on canvas 46x27. Petit Palais, Geneva.

223. *The Laundress* (*La blanchisseuse*) (fig. 9), 1894. Oil on canvas 46.5x27.5. Petit Palais, Geneva.

224. *Woman Fixing her Hair* (*Femme déshabillée se coiffant*), 1895. Charcoal and pastel 63x51. Petit Palais, Geneva.

225. *Mother and Child with Cat* (*Mère et enfant avec chat*) (plate 15), 1895. Oil on canvas 90x58.3. Study for C.494. Petit Palais, Geneva.

226. *The 14th of July* (*Le 14 juillet*), 1895. Oil on canvas 38x46. Petit Palais, Geneva.

227. *Young Woman of the Street (Jeune fille de la rue)* (plate 18, front cover), ca. 1895. Oil on canvas 81x60. Petit Palais, Geneva.

228. *Village in a Rainstorm (Le village sous l'orage)*, 1895. Oil on canvas 65x80. Petit Palais, Geneva.

229. *Leaving the Theatre (Sortie du théâtre)*, 1902. Oil on canvas 100x65. Petit Palais, Geneva.

230. *The Windmills of Montmartre (Les moulins de Montmartre)* (fig. 10), 1903. Oil on canvas 66x95. Petit Palais, Geneva.

231. *Two Cats Reclining on the Sofa (Deux chats allongés sur le sofa)*, 1908. Oil on canvas 66x82. Petit Palais, Geneva.

232. *Idyll (L'idylle)*, 1909. Oil on canvas 81x60.5. Petit Palais, Geneva.

Bronzes

233. *Two Cats Crouching (Deux chats se tournant le dos)*, ca. 1904. Bronze 19x16. Mrs. Susan Schimmel Goldstein.

234. *Cat Reclining on a Square Stand (Grand chat couché sur un socle carré)*, ca. 1904. Bronze 16x16. Mrs. Susan Schimmel Goldstein.

235. *Reclining Cat*, ca. 1904. Bronze 23x12. Margot Flatau.

236. *Cat Sitting on a Stand (Chat assis sur socle)*, ca. 1904. Bronze 24. Norma Bartman.

237. *Cat Reclining on a Rectangular Stand (Chat couché sur socle rectangulaire)*, ca. 1904. Bronze 23x11. Norma Bartman.

238. *Cat reclining on a Stand (Chat couché sur socle)*, ca. 1904, Bronze 13x6.5. Norma Bartman.

Wood Blocks

239. *Desire*, 1897. Wood block, 11x5.8. Actual wood block for *L'image* (C.678). Carved by Thévenin. Mr. and Mrs. Herbert D. Schimmel.

Two Nude Models, 1902, softground etching (cat. 15).

Plate 19. *Yvette Guilbert Ambassadeurs*, 1894,
color lithographic poster (cat. 76).

Plate 20. *Pure Sterilized Milk from the Vingeanne Region*, 1894, color lithographic poster (cat. 74).

Woman Fixing her Hair, 1895, charcoal and pastel (cat. 224).

Bibliography

Exhibition Catalogs

1894. *Première Exposition de l'oeuvre dessinée et peinte de T.A. Steinlen.* Paris: Bodinière [Gallery], 10 Apr.-15 May.

1903. France, Anatole. Preface to *Exposition d'ouvrages peints, dessinés, ou gravés par Th.-A. Steinlen.* Paris: E. Pelletan, Nov.-Dec.

1914. *Steinlen.* London: Leicester Galleries, May-June.

1917. Galerie La Boetie. *Exposition Steinlen.* Paris: Editions la Guerre.

1919. Gallatin, A.E. *Forain and Steinlen, Drawings and Lithographs.* First American exhibition. New York: Arden Gallery, 14-28 Jan.

1953. *Théophile Alexandre Steinlen, 1859-1923.* Paris: Bibliothèque nationale, May-June.

1954. *Steinlen.* London: Arts Council of Great Britain.

1960. *An Exhibition of Drawings, Etchings, Lithographs by Théophile-Alexandre Steinlen.* London: Editions Graphiques.

1963. Leiris, Alain de. Introduction to *Théophile-Alexandre Steinlen.* New York: Charles E. Slatkin Galleries, 18 Oct.-16 Nov.

1964. *Expositia Steinlen.* Bucharest: Muzeul de Arta al Republicii Populara Romania, May-June.

1965. *Steinlen* Brussels: Galerie Brachot, 23 Sept.-5 Oct.

1966. Damadian, L. *Steinlen.* Bucharest: Muzuel de Arta al Republicii Socialiste Romania, May-June.

1968. *Steinlen.* London: Ferrers [Gallery].

1968. Viatte, Francoise. *Dessins de Steinlen, 1859-1923.* Paris: Musée national du Louvre, Cabinet des Dessins.

1970. *Rétrospective Théophile-Alexandre Steinlen.* Charleroi: Palais des beaux-arts, 24 Oct.-22 Nov.

1973. Steinlen, Marguerite. *Steinlen: Peintures et Dessins.* Saint-Denis: Musée Municipal d'Art et d'Histoire, 5 Oct.-18 Nov.

1974. Galerie des Arts Décoratifs. *Théophile-Alexandre Steinlen: Huiles, pastels, dessins, estampes, affiches, sculptures.* Lausanne: Editions Gad, 13 Dec. 1973-2 Feb.

1976. *Steinlen.* Neuss, Germany: Clemens-Sels Museum, Oct.-Dec.

1977. *Steinlen 1859-1923.* Moscow: Pushkin Museum.

1977. Steinlen, Marguerite. *Alexandre-Théophile Steinlen.* Paris: Musée de Montmartre, June-Sept.

1978. *Théophile-Alexandre Steinlen, 1859-1923.* Warsaw: Muzeum Nardowe.

1978. *Théophile Alexandre Steinlen. Gemälde, Zeichnungen, Graphik, Bronzen.* Hamburg: Galerie XX.

1978. *Théophile-Alexandre Steinlen, 1859-1923.* Berlin: Staatliche Kunsthalle, 15 Jan.-15 Feb.

1978. *Michele Castel—Alexandre Steinlen.* Denges-prés-Lausanne: Galerie d'Arfi, June.

1978. *Théophile-Alexandre Steinlen.* Albi: Musée Toulouse-Lautrec, 27 June-15 Sept.

1979. *Th. A. Steinlen.* Stuttgart: Kunsthaus Buhler, 5-28 Feb.

1979. *Th.-A. Steinlen.* Geneva: Petit Palais, L'Orangerie, 28 Nov.

1980. *Théophile-Alexandre Steinlen.* Turin: Galleria Civica d'Arte Moderna, May-July.

1981. Frèrebeau-O'Berthur, Mariel. *Centenaire du Cabaret du chat noir.* Paris: Musée de Montmartre.

General Bibliography

Abdy, Jane. *The French Poster: Cheret to Cappiello.* London: Studio Vista, 1969.

Alexandre, Arsène. *L'Art du rire et de la caricature.* Paris: May & Motteroz, 1892.

Alexandre, Arsène; Bunner, H.C.; Jaccaci, August; and Spielmann, M.H. *The Modern Poster.* New York: Charles Scribner's, 1895.

Appelbaum, Stanley. *French Satirical Drawings from "L'Assiette au Beurre".* New York: 1978.

Appelbaum, Stanley. *Simplicissimus. 180 Satirical Drawings from the Famous German Weekly.* New York: 1975.

Appignanesi, Lisa. *The Cabaret.* New York: Universe Books, 1976.

L'Art au service de la paix. Geneva: Petit Palais, 1970.

"Artistic French Lithographs." *The Poster* no. 1, Nov. 1898, pp. 192-94.

Arwas, Victor. *Affiches et gravures de la belle epoque.* Paris: Flammarion, 1978. [English edition: *Belle Epoque: Posters & Graphics.* London: Academy/New York: Rizzoli, 1978.]

Atelier Th.A. Steinlen. Vente Après Décès: Catalogue des aquarelles-dessins estampes de Steinlen. Paris: Hôtel Drouot, 29-30 Apr. 1925.

L'Aube du XXe siècle. Peintres de Montmartre. Geneva: Petit Palais, ca. 1968.

L'*Aube du XXe siécle de Renoir a Chagall*. Geneva: Petit Palais, 1968.

Auriol, Georges. "Steinlen." *Les Arts français* 3 (1917), 43-48.

Auriol, Georges, and Dyssord, Jacques. *Steinlen et la rue, Saint-Lazare*. Paris: E. Rey, 1930.

Aveline, Claude. *Steinlen: L'Homme & l'oeuvre*. Paris: Les Ecrivains Reunis, 1926.

Averill, Esther. "Steinlen and Pelletan: An Artist and His Publisher." *Horn Book Magazine* 13 (1937): 45-52.

Bairati, Eleanora; Falkus, Malcolm; Jullian, Phillipe; Monelli, Paolo; Riesz, Janos; and Vigezzi, Brunello. *La Belle Epoque. Fifteen Euphoric Years of European History*. New York: William Morrow, 1978.

Barnicoat, John. *A Concise History of Posters*. London: Thames & Hudson, 1972.

Baruch, Hugo [Jack Bilbo]. *Toulouse-Lautrec and Steinlen*. London: Modern Art Gallery, 1946.

Bauch, Kurt. Introduction to *Jugendstil. Der Weg Ins 20. Jahrhundert*. Heidelberg/Munich: Keysersche, 1969.

Benedite, Léonce. "Alexandre Steinlen." *Die Graphischen Kunste* 21 (1898): 83-88.

Beraldi, Henri. *Les Graveurs du XIXe siècle: Guide de l'amateur d'estampes modernes*. Volume 12. Paris: Conquet, 1885-92.

Blunt, Anthony, and Pool, Phoebe. *Picasso, The Formative Years: A Study of His Sources*. Greenwich: New York Graphic Society, 1962.

Bouvy, Eugène. "Steinlen." *Amateur d'Estampes* 3(1924): 1-10.

Bouyer, Raymond. "Le musique illustrée, Steinlen." *L'Art Décoratif*, Oct. 1901, pp. 1-8.

Brisson, Adolphe. *Nos Humoristes: Caran d'Ache, J.L. Forain, Hermann-Paul, Léandre, Robida, Steinlen, Willette*. Paris: Société d'Edition Artistique, 1900.

Broido, Lucy. *French Opera Posters, 1868-1930*. New York: Dover, 1976.

Brown, Milton W. *American Painting from the Armory Show to the Depression*. Princeton: Princeton University Press, 1955.

Bruneteaux, Léon. "Alexandre Steinlen, dessinateur, lithographe, peintre." *Société Nouvelle* 2 (1907): 295-302.

Cabanne, Pierre. *Pablo Picasso. His Life and Times*. Translated by Harold J. Salemson. New York: William Morrow, 1977.

Le *Café-Concert: Affiches de la Bibliotheque du Musée des Arts Décoratifs. 1870-1914*. Paris: Musée des Arts Décoratifs, 1978.

Catalogue des dessins rehaussés par Steinlen. Paris: Hôtel Drouot, 1907.

Catalogue des tableaux, aquarelles, dessins, eaux-fortes, pointes-sèches, lithographies par Th.-A. Steinlen. Paris: Hôtel Drouot, 1930-31.

Catalogue de tableaux et dessins, oeuvres importantes de Toulous-Lautrec, dessins originaux de Steinlen, por l'illustration des oeuvres de Aristide Bruant. Paris: Hôtel Drouot, 1905.

Cate, Phillip Dennis, and Hitchings, Sinclair Hamilton. *The Color Revolution. Color Lithography in France, 1890-1900*. Salt Lake City: Peregrine Smith, 1978.

Cate, Phillip Dennis. "Empathy with the Humanity of the Streets." *ARTnews*, Mar. 1977, pp. 56-59.

Cate, Phillip Dennis, "La Plume and Its Salon des Cent." *Print Review* 8 (1978): 61-68.

Cate, Phillip Dennis. "The Revolutionary Intrigue among 19th Century Printmakers." *ARTnews*, Mar. 1978.

Cats by Steinlen and Nam. London: Ferrers Gallery, Mar. 1971.

"Les Chats de Steinlen." *Amateur d'Estampes* 5 (1926): 29-30.

Cleaver, James. *A History of Graphic Art*. New York: Philosophical Library, 1963.

Clément-Janin, Noël. "Steinlen." *Die Graphischen Künste* 3 (1906): 66-72.

Clément-Janin, Noël. "Steinlen." *Print Collector's Quarterly* 18 (1931): 33-35.

Clément-Janin, Noël. "Un Grand Editeur: Pelletan." *Byblis* 8 (1929): 126-141.

Cleveland Museum of Art; Rutgers University Art Gallery; and Walters Art Gallery. *Japonisme: Japanese Influence on French Art, 1854-1910*. Rutland/Tokyo: Charles E. Tuttle, 1975.

Constantine, Mildred. *Word and Image*. New York: Museum of Modern Art, 1968.

Contat-Mercanton, Leonie. *Théophile-Alexandre Steinlen, 1859-1923*. Berne: Edition du Musée Gutenberg Suisse 1959.

Crauzat, Ernest de. "Le Chanson des gueux et les dernières chansons de Steinlen." *L'Art Decoratif*, Sept. 1910, pp. 107-112.

Crauzat, Ernest de. "Les 'incises' de Steinlen." *Byblis* 5 (1926): pp. 31-38.

Crauzat, Ernest de. *L'Oeuvre grave et lithographie de Steinlen*. Paris: Société de Propagation des Livres d'Art, 1913.

Crauzat, Ernest de. "Steinlen . . . ." *Les Maîtres Illustrateurs* 9 (1902): 1,3,37.

Crauzat, Ernest de. "Th.-A. Steinlen, artiste montmartrois." *Byblis* 6 (1927): 127-138.

Crespelle, J.-P. *Montmartre Vivant*. Paris: Hachette, 1964.

Davis, Richard Harding. *About Paris*. New York: Harper & Bros., 1895.

Deberdt, Raoul. *La Caricature et l'humour français au XIXme siècle*. Paris: Librairie Larousse, ca. 1898.

Delteil, Löys. *Manuel de l'amateur d'estampes des XIXe et XXe siècles. (1801-1924)*. Paris: Dorbon-Aîné, 1925.

Deverin, Edouard. "Steinlen et son temps." *L'Art et Les Artistes*, Dec. 1933, pp. 97-101.

Duverney, Paul. "A Chat with Steinlen." *The Poster*, Dec. 1898, pp. 249-252.

Edouard-Joseph, Rene *Dictionnaire biographique des artistes contemporains, 1910-1930*. Paris: Librairie Grund, 1934.

Edwards, George Wharton. *Paris*. Philadelphia: Penn Publishing Co., 1924.

Egbert, Donald Drew. *Social Radicalism and the Arts: Western Europe*. New York: Knopf, 1970.

Eichenberg, Fritz. *The Art of the Print: Masterpieces, History, Techniques*. New York: Abrams, 1976.

Emanuel, Frank L. *The Illustrators of Montmartre*. The Langham Series of Art Monographs, vol. 3. London: A. Siegle, 1904.

English & French Drawings & Steinlen Drawings. London: Browse & Darby Gallery, 1980.

L'Estampe et l'affiche, 3 volumes. Paris: Edouard Pelletan, 1897-1899.

Exhibition of Contemporary French Prints. Washington, D.C.: Library of Congress, 1928.

"Exhibition of War Posters from the Frank M. Gregg Collection." *The Bulletin*, Sept.-Oct. 1917, pp. 113-116.

Fels, Florent. *L'Art vivant de 1900 a nos jours*. Geneva: Pierre Cailler, 1950.

Fierens-Gevaert, H. "Un Maitre affichiste— Steinlen." *Art et Decoration*, July 1897, pp. 17-22.

Forgotton Printmakers of the 19th Century. Chicago: Kovler Gallery, 1967-68.

France, Anatole. "L'oeuvre de Steinlen." *Annales Politiques et Littéraires* 64 (1920): pp. 35-37.

Frèrebeau, Mariel. "What is Montmartre? Nothing! What should it be? Everything!" *ARTnews*, Mar. 1977, pp. 60-62.

From Renoir to Chagall. Geneva: Petit Palais, 1979.

Gallatin, Albert Eugene. *Art and the Great War*. New York: Dutton, 1919.

Gallatin, Albert Eugene. "Steinlen." *Art and Progress* 7 (1915): 23-24.

Gill, Susan. "Steinlen's Prints: Social Imagery in Late 19th Century Graphic Art." *Print Collector's Newsletter*, Mar. 1979, pp. 8-12.

Glaser, Kurt. *Graphik der Neuzeit*. Berlin: Bruno Cassirer, 1922.

Gute, Herbert. *Th.A. Steinlen, Vermächtnis*. Berlin: Henschelverlag, 1954.

Haftmann, Werner. *Painting in the Twentieth Century*. New York: Praeger, 1960.

Harthan, John. *The History of the Illustrated Book: The Western Tradition*. London/New York: Thames & Hudson, 1981.

Hartmann, Sadakichi. *Japanese Art*. Boston: L.C. Page, 1904.

Herbert, Eugenia. *The Artist and Social Reform: France and Belgium, 1885-1898*. New Haven: Yale University Press, 1961.

Herbert, Robert, and Herbert, Eugenia W. "Artists & Anarchism: Unpublished Letters of Pissarro, Signac & Others - I." *Burlington Magazine*, Nov. 1960, pp. 473-82.

Hiatt, Charles. *Picture Posters*. London: George Bell, 1895.

Hillier, Bevis. *Posters*. New York: Stein & Day, 1969.

Hofer, Phillip. Introduction to *The Artist and the Book, 1860-1960, in Western Europe and the United States*. Cambridge: Harvard College Library, Department of Printing and Graphic Arts, 1961.

Holme, Charles. *Modern Pen Drawings: European and American*. London: The Studio, 1901.

Holme, Charles, ed. *Pen, Pencil and Chalk*. London: The Studio, 1911.

Huguenin, L.H. "Théophile Alexandre Steinlen." *Cahiers D'Art-documents* 124 (1960): 1-16.

Inghelbrecht, Germaine. *D.E. Inghelbrecht et son temps*. Neuchatel: A la Baconniere, 1978.

Jacob, Alain. "Affiches: Art et publicité." *ABC Decor*, Oct. 1979, pp. 47-58.

Jones, Sydney R. *Posters & Their Designers*. Edited by Geoffrey Holme. London: The Studio, 1924.

Jourdain, Francis. "Théophile-Alexandre Steinlen." *Buchkunst* 4 (1963): pp. 7-32.

Jourdain, Francis. *Un Grand Imagier: Alexandre Steinlen*. Paris: Editions Cercle d'Art, 1954.

Jullian, Philippe. *Montmartre*. Translated by Anne Carter. Oxford: Phaidon/New York: Dutton, 1977.

Klagebusch, H. "Théophile Alexandre Steinlen." *Kunst das Schöne Heim*, Nov. 1977, pp. 668-71.

Kollwitz, Käthe. *The Diary and Letters*. Translated by Richard and Clara Winston. Chicago: Henry Regnery, 1955.

Lauer, Leo. *Steinlen: Vier en Twintig Platen*. Amsterdam: Vennootschap Letteren en Kunst, 1907. [English edition: *Steinlen and His Art*. London: Chatto & Windus, 1911.]

Laver, James. *XIXth Century French Posters*. London: Nicholson & Watson, 1944.

Leclerc, Emile. "Steinlen." *Papyrus*, Apr. 1924, pp. 249-52.

Le Comte, Georges. *Steinlen: Chats et autres bêtes: Dessins inedits*. Paris: Eugene Rey, 1933.

Lenoir, Maurice. "Steinlen et son oeuvre." *Le Mirliton*, 15 Dec. 1895, pp. 2-3.

Lewandowski, Herbert. *Das Sexualproblem in der Modern Literatur und Kunst*. Dresden: Paul Aretz, 1927.

Lewis, John. *The Twentieth Century Book: Its Illustration and Design*. London: Studio Vista, 1967.

Lucas, E.V. *A Wanderer in Paris*. London: Meuthen, 1909.

Maillard, Léon. *Les Menus & programmes illutrés*. Paris: Librairie Aristique, 1898.

Maitres connus et méconnus de Montmartre à Montparnasse. Geneva: Oscar Ghez, June-Sept. 1964.

Maloney, William E., ed. *The Illustrated Cat*. New York: A Push Pin Press, Harmony Books, 1976.

Marguery, Henry. "Les Chats dans l'oeuvre de Steinlen." *Amateur D'Estampes* 7 (1928): pp. 47-53.

Mauclair, Camille. "A Travers Les Ateliers d'artistes: Steinlen." *L'Art et les Artistes*, Sept. 1907, pp. 297-303.

Mauclair, Camille. *La Beauté des formes*. Paris: Librairie Universelle 1927.

Mauclair, Camille. "La Guerre par Steinlen." *L'art et les Artistes*, Mar. 1918.

Mery, Fernand. *The Life, History and Magic of the Cat*. Translated by Emma Street. New York: Grosset & Dunlap, 1968.

Metzl, Ervine. *The Poster: Its History and Its Art*. New York: Watson-Guptill, 1963.

Morin, Louis. "Steinlen." *L'Oeuvre et L'Image*, Oct. 1901.

Mourey, Gabriel. "Coloured Etchings in France (First Article)." *The Studio*, 15 Feb. 1901, pp. 3-14.

Mourey, Gabriel. "The Illustrators of Music." *The Studio*, 15 Oct. 1898, pp. 86-98.

Mourey, Gabriel. "Some French Illustrated Theatre Programmes." *The Studio*, 15 Feb. 1897, pp. 237-43.

Mourey, Gabriel. "Steinlen As a Lithographer." *The Studio*, 15 Oct. 1897, pp. 251-59.

Mueller, Max. *Frankreich im Kriege, 1914-1916*. Zurich: Art Institut Orell Füssli, 1917.

Muller, Frederik. *Catalogue des 125 dessins par Th.A. Steinlen*. Amsterdam: Mardi, 1912.

Müller, Hermann Alexander, and Singer, Hans W. *Allgemeines Künstler-Lexicon. Leben und Werke der Berühmsten Bildenen Künstler*. Frankfurt: Rütten, 1921-22.

Nevill, Ralph. *Days and Nights in Montmartre and the Latin Quarter*. New York: George H. Doran, 1927.

Oeuvre dessinée de Steinlen. Paris: Hôtel Drouot, 1970.

Oeuvre graphique de Steinlen. Paris: Hôtel Drouot, 1971.

"L'Oeuvre de Th.-A. Steinlen." *Gazette des Beaux Arts*, Oct. 1913, pp. 299-301.

Penfield, Edward. *Posters in Miniature*. London: John Lane/New York: R.H. Russell & Son, 1896.

Pennell, Joseph. *The Graphic Arts*. Chicago: University of Chicago, 1921.

Pennell, Joseph, and Pennell, Elizabeth Robins. *Lithography & Lithographers. Some Chapters in the Art*. New York: Century/London: T. Fisher Unwin, 1898.

Pfefferkorn, R. "Théophile Alexandre Steinlen." *Graphische Kunst* 11 (1978): pp. 54-57.

Pianzola, Maurice. *Théophile-Alexandre Steinlen*. Lausanne: Editions Recontre, 1971.

Pica, Vittorio. "Théophile-Alexandre Steinlen." *Emporium* 28 (1908): pp. 245-62.

Pichon, Leon. *The New Book-Illustration in France*. Translated by Herbert B. Grimsditch. London: The Studio, 1924.

Price, Charles Marlack. *Posters. A Critical Study of the Development of Poster Design in Continental Europe, England and America*. New York: George W. Bricka, 1913.

Puech, Lucien. "Steinlen in time." *L'Album*. Apr. 1902.

Rainov, Bogomil. *Aleksandur Stainlen; Monografiia*. Sofia: Bulgarski khudozhnik, 1962.

Rath Museum. *The Painters of Montmartre and Montparnasse from Renoir to Valtat*. Geneva: Oscar Ghez/New York: Shorewood, 1965.

Reynolds, Graham. *Nineteenth Century Drawings, 1850-1900*. London: Pleiades Books, 1949.

Rickards, Maurice. *Banned Posters*. Park Ridge: Noyes Press, 1972.

Rickards, Maurice. *Posters of the First World War*. New York: Walker, 1968.

Rickards, Maurice. *The Rise and Fall of the Poster*. New York: McGraw-Hill, 1971.

Roberts-Jones, Philippe. *De Daumier à Lautrec*. Paris: Les Beaux-Arts, 1960.

Roger-Marx, Claude. *French Original Engravings From Manet to the Present Time*. London: Hyperion Press, 1939.

Roger-Marx, Claude. *Graphic Art of the 19th Century*. Translated by E. M. Gwyer. New York: McGraw-Hill, 1962.

Romi. *Petite Histoire des cafés-concerts parisiens*. Paris: Jean Chitry et Cie, 1950.

Rosenthal, Mark. *Simplicissimus. The Art of Germany's Most Influential Satire Magazine (1896-1944)*. New York: Die Aktion Productions, 1979.

Royer, Jean-Michel. *Le Livre d'or de l'assiette au beurre I. 1901-1906*. Paris: Jean-Claude Simoën, 1977.

Rudorff, Raymond. *The Belle Epoque. Paris in the Nineties*. New York: Saturday Review Press, 1972.

Sachs, Hans. "Théophile Alexandre Steinlen." *Der Cicerone*, June 1924, pp. 483-94.

Sachs, Hans. "Théophile Alexandre Steinlen." *Jahrbuch der Jungen Kunst*, 1924, pp. 440-55.

St. John, Bruce. *John Sloan*. New York: Praeger, 1971.

Salaman, Malcolm C. *Modern Woodcuts and Lithographs by British and French Artists*. London: The Studio, 1919.

Salanon, René, and Samson, Claude. *Cent Ans d'affiches "La Belle Epoque."* Paris: Bibliothèque des Arts Décoratifs, 1964.

Santier, Maxmiliano. "Steinlen, Pintor de los Humildes." *Pluma*, July 1930, pp. 61-82.

Schardt, Hermann. *Paris 1900. Masterworks of French Poster Art*. New York: Putnam and Sons, 1970.

Shikes, Ralph E. *The Indignant Eye. The Artist as Social Critic in Prints and Drawings from the Fifteenth Century to Picasso*. Boston: Beacon Press, 1969.

Sidorov, Aleksei Alekseevich. *Steinlen, Khudozhnik Parizhskogo Proletariata*. Moscow: Gos. izd-vo, 1919.

Singer, Hans W. *Handbuch für Kupferstichsammler. Technische Erklärungen Ratschläge für das Sammeln und das Aufbewahren*. Leipzig: Karl W. Hiersemann, 1922.

Singer, Hans W. *Die Moderne Graphik*. Leipzig: E.A. Seemann, 1920.

"Some Drawings by Steinlen." *The Studio*, 15 Feb. 1899, pp. 18-25.

Springer, Annemarie. "Terrorism and Anarchy: Late 19th Century Images of a Political Phenomenon in France." *Art Journal*, Summer 1979, pp. 261-66.

"Steinlen." *The Studio*, 15 Feb. 1897, pp. 196-97.

Steinlen, 1859-1923. Paris: Maison de la pensée francaise, 1960-61.

Steinlen and His Art. London: Chatto & Windus, 1911.

"Steinlen écrit à sa mère." *Du*, May 1953, p. 32.

Steinlen, Marguerite. "Steinlen." *Du*, May 1953, pp. 18-31.

Steinlen, Théophile-Alexandre. *Steinlen Cats: Drawings*. New York: Dover, 1980.

Steinlen, Théophile-Alexandre. *Steinlen's Drawings 126 Plates from "Gil Blas illustré"*. New York: Dover, 1980.

Sterner, Gabriele. *Jugenstil. Kunstformen Zwischen Individualismus und Massengesellschaft*. Cologne: M. DuMont Schuberg, 1975.

"Studio-Talk: Paris." *The Studio*, 15 Feb. 1900, pp. 58-60.

Taylor, Francis Henry. "Steinlen and Zola: Realism with a Purpose." *Parnassus*, May 1931, pp. 3-5.

"Théophile-Alexandre Steinlen, 1859-1923." *Cahier de l'art mineur*, Sept. 1976.

"Théophile Alexandre Steinlen, 1859-1923." *Gebrauchsgraphik*, Nov. 1930, pp. 24-35.

Thompson, Jan. "The Role of Women in the Iconography of Art Nouveau." *Art Journal*, Winter 1971-1972, pp. 158-67.

Thon, Christina. *Französische Plakate des 19. Jahrhunderts*. Berlin: Kunstbibliothek, 1968.

Valotaire, M. "Théophile Alexandre Steinlen." *The Studio*, Mar. 1924, pp. 123-27.

Van Vorst, Maria. *Modern French Masters*. Paris:/New York: Brentano's, 1904.

Vollard, Ambroise. *Recollections of a Picture Dealer*. Translated by Violet M. MacDonald. New York: Dover, 1978.

Warnod, André. *Les Berceaux de la jeune peinture: Montmartre, Montparnasse*. Paris: Albin Michel, ca. 1923.

Weill, Alain. *Art Nouveau Postcards. The Posterists' Postcards*. New York: Images Graphiques, 1977.

Weill, Alain. *Masters of the Poster 1896-1900*. New York: Images Graphiques, 1977.

Weill, Alain. *100 Years of Posters of the Folies Bergère and Music Halls of Paris*. New York: Images Graphiques, 1977.

Weisberg, Gabriel P. *Images of Women: Printmakers in France from 1830-1930*. Salt Lake City: University of Utah, 1978.

Weisberg, Gabriel P. *Social Concern and the Worker: French Prints from 1830-1910*. Salt Lake City: University of Utah, 1974.

Wember, Paul. *Die Jungend der Plakate, 1887-1917*. Krefeld: Scherpe Verlag, 1961.

Wilenski, R.H. *Modern French Painters*. 4th ed. London: Faber & Faber, 1963.

Wintsch, Jean. *Un Artiste lausannois: Steinlen*. Lausanne: Armand Lapie, 1919.

Index